The
Encyclopedia
of
Popular
Misconceptions

The Encyclopedia of Popular Misconceptions

Ferris Johnsen

A CITADEL PRESS BOOK
Published by Carol Publishing Group

A Citadel Press Book
Published by Carol Publishing Group
Citadel Press is a registered trademark of Carol Communications, Inc.
Editorial Offices: 600 Madison Avenue, New York, N.Y. 10022
Sales and Distribution Offices: 120 Enterprise Avenue, Secaucus, N.J. 07094
In Canada: Canadian Manda Group, P.O. Box 920, Station U, Toronto, Ontario M8Z 5P9
Queries regarding rights and permissions should be addressed to Carol Publishing Group, 600 Madison Avenue, New York, N.Y. 10022

Carol Publishing Group books are available at special discounts for bulk purchases, sales promotions, fund raising, or educational purposes. Special editions can be created to specifications. For details, contact Special Sales Department, Carol Publishing Group, 120 Enterprise Avenue, Secaucus, N.J. 07094

Manufactured in the United States of America

10 9 8 7 6 5 4 3 2 1

Library of Congress Cataloging-in-Publication Data

Johnsen, Ferris.
  The encyclopedia of popular misconceptions : the ultimate debunker's guide to widely accepted fallacies / by Ferris Johnsen.
    p.   cm.
  "A Citadel Press book."
  ISBN 0-8065-1556-2
  1. Errors, Popular—Dictionaries.   I. Title.
AZ999.J64   1994
001.9′6—dc20   94-18196
                                                      CIP

Foreword

I often look back on my college experience marveling, not so much that I passed my courses, but that my old misfiring Pontiac was able to deliver me each day to the distant campus. The old horse needed a tuneup and a spark plug or two but that was a luxury my penurious pocket wouldn't allow. But despite its physiomechanical faults we both persevered and I managed to graduate. Over the years I have learned that most of us torque in the world with a few bad spark plugs, somehow surviving despite the many specious assumptions that turn out to be embarrassingly wrong, and oftimes rather harmful. Some people become quite discombobulated when caught with misinformation, others only mildly so or not at all. I confess, I find myself, woefully, in the former category—learning that a long-held belief is not really a fact of life gives me a feeling of being had.

Quite probably, my penchant for sleuthing the true-false issue came from a freshman-year professor who insisted that all his students get a second opinion on almost everything—from lectures, discussions, books, encyclopedias, and, yea verily, even the Bible itself with its many translations. So, if I learned little else from him, I picked up on that neurotic habit, which is why I undertook to write this book. Even in my research for the book, just when I thought I had an indisputable fact at a dead end, a brighter light would sometimes turn on and expose yet another faulty fact. Sometimes my neurosis causes me anguish but most of the time it helps clear the air. Socrates was the first real questioner and look what happened to him!

Because I enjoy humor in virtually all literature, the reader will find a sprinkling of it throughout this work, but it isn't easy to inject humor into an encyclopedic format; some subjects simply refuse to be burlesqued. Therefore, some of the entries will have to remain prosaic and sterile. Also, those readers on the smart side of the bell curve are going to wonder why I've included entries that even old-world monkeys would have little trouble with. I must beg their indulgence, because misconceptions reach into every stratum of literacy and are no respecters of persons.

Finally, as to acknowledgments regarding this book, suffice it to say it was an eclectic undertaking, with material coming from sources too numerous to list—most of it just laborious trench work. I suppose my best help, however, would have to be the zillion shelved books in our wonderful city and county libraries whose pages bear my determined fingerprints, in addition to the many patient librarians who gave me more than the time of day with their expert assistance. Surely, they must have hated to see me coming.

The Encyclopedia of Popular Misconceptions

A

ABACUS AND OTHER COUNTING DEVICES

Despite our tendency to equate the crude counting device—the abacus—with Japan and China, the beady contrivance is not an original invention of any Oriental country. The particular mechanism they use to tally up their rice balls and fish cakes is actually the "soroban," which made its appearance very late on the scene—about 1500 A.D. The original, even more crude, abacus dates back to the Egyptians, who were using it at least by the year 2000 B.C. Even the ropey Radio-Shack version used by the Incas of South America—the quipu—antedated the Oriental abacus.

ABNER DOUBLEDAY INVENTED BASEBALL?

If ever there was an all-American, apple-pie innovation it is our cherished game of baseball. Yes, we love it but, contrary to almost everyone's belief, we didn't invent it. Seasoned history tells us that an American army officer, Abner Doubleday, started the game of baseball in a Cooperstown, New York, field in 1839; however, a plethora of new evidence throws a fastball curve at the Doubleday-Cooperstown connection in a very convincing fashion. In the beginning days of U.S. baseball, there was little to suggest that baseball was anything but a spinoff from the popular English children's game known as "rounders." So vague and tenuous was the idea of baseball originating in this country that a commission

1

was established (at the instigation of A. G. Spalding, a sporting-goods tycoon) to prove its exclusively U.S. origin. The commission, heavily weighted with vested interests, declared in 1908 that Doubleday, a hero of the Battle of Gettysburg, was indeed the inventor of the game of baseball. At the time, who cared? It wasn't until 1939 that Robert W. Henderson of the New York Public Library issued a written refutation of the Doubleday theory that put baseball back on the playgrounds of Great Britain. Further evidence surfaced showing the use of the term "baseball" in England as early as the first half of the eighteenth century. In 1744 *A Little Pretty Pocket-Book* was published in England and convincingly illustrated the actual game of baseball being played. The popular book was published in America in 1762 and again in 1787. A more telling book was published in London in 1823 entitled *The Boy's Own Book.* It was a treatise on boys' sports and their rules, which included a chapter on the original English game of rounders. There is more, much more, including the 1977 Encyclopedia of Sports article written by Frank Menke who, after considerable research, concluded: "Not only did Doubleday not invent baseball, he probably never even played it." All other evidence aside, the capstone proof may be that in Abner Doubleday's own memoirs, baseball isn't even mentioned. If you invented baseball, would you strike yourself out of the history books?

ABOLITIONIST MOVEMENT
The abolitionist movement is generally thought to refer only to the termination of slavery and the slave trade in the United States during the nineteenth century. But there were anti-slavery agitations long before those normally written about in modern textbooks. The Quakers and other disturber groups were righteously railing against the practice of slavery even in colonial times, and in the northern states slavery was virtually eliminated before the word *abolitionist* came into being.

ABRAHAM, HIS WIVES AND CHILDREN

Most casual readers of the Old Testament are aware that Abraham, first of the Hebrew patriarchs, was ordained by the Lord to become a father at the unlikely age of one hundred years with his aged wife Sarah. But in the minds of most people there seems to be the assumption that Abraham's fathering came to a halt after Isaac's birth and Sarah's death. Actually, the "Father of Nations" was really just hitting his libidinal prime when Isaac was born. Chapter 25 of the Book of Genesis tells us: "Then again Abraham took a wife and her name was Keturah. And she bare him Zimran, Jokshan, and Medan, and Midian, and Ishbak, and Shuah." Father Abraham lived to be 175, and was prolific many years beyond the century mark.

ABSOLUTE ZERO

It is a generally accepted notion that "absolute zero" is the lowest possible temperature that can be achieved, a temperature so cold that atoms pack it in and become motionless. (Heating, on the other hand, throws atoms into a motion panic.) However, the idea that all the molecular marbles cease to budge at absolute zero is not true; only that no molecular motion is available for *transfer* to other systems at that temperature. It would therefore be more accurate to say there is no thermal energy at absolute zero.

ACCOUNTANTS

Most people are aware that CPAs must be board-certified before they can work as certified public accountants. What isn't generally known, however, is that accountants without board certification (and with marginal practical experience) can work in public accounting as long as they don't call themselves CPAs. Apparently they don't mind the ignominy if it's green enough.

ACTS OF THE APOSTLES
There has always been controversy concerning the authorship of some of the books of the Bible. The book of the "Acts
of the Apostles" comes to mind. Who wrote it? Lay church
members usually credit Paul as having written it, but it is
clear that *Luke* was the author of Acts. The problem is, we
have to refer to two scriptures in two different books to prove
it: Acts 1:1,2 and Luke 1:3,4. In these scriptures, Luke is
attempting to reinforce his testimony concerning the
efficacy of Christ's ministry, thus proving conclusively that he
was indeed the book's author.

ACUPUNCTURE
As technical and complicated as the practice of acupuncture
is, most people suppose it to be regulated, which it is not. At
least, in most states it is not (California and New York being
the exceptions). With that in mind, just remember, the next
time you submit to being pincushioned with all those menacing darts, the practitioner may be doing just that—
practicing!

AFRICAN VIOLET
That lovely tropical plant you've got hanging in your living
room, and which you've always called an African violet, is not
really a violet at all, but a relative of the gloxinia. But don't
stop calling it an African violet, because who can remember
its real name—*Saintpaulia?* While you're at it, you can also
impress your friends by telling them that your violet is really
an herb.

AIRCRAFT OF THE ARMED SERVICES
Here's one for the afterburner: Notwithstanding the Air
Force's mission—to achieve strategic and tactical superiority
through air power—it is the U.S. Army that has the most
aircraft. This is due to the large number of light and
ultralight aircraft assigned for reconnaissance and troop
support, including a large fleet of choppers.

AIR POCKETS

A total vacuum might qualify as being an "air pocket," but not those up-and-down drafts that passengers experience midway through their in-flight meal at 20,000 feet. In short, there is no such thing as an air pocket, but it's still a good idea to keep your seat buckled during your hastily served flight meal.

AIR SAFETY

It is a fallacy that air travel is not as safe as it has been in the past, and that airplane crashes are increasing. This unfounded consensus, according to the National Aviation Safety Institute, is as false as the notion that air crashes always come in threes. According to the institute, there were 31 million scheduled departures during the period 1983 to 1987, with only 107 accidents (its official definition of an accident being "any occurrence associated with either a fatal or serious injury to passengers or crew, or significant damage to the aircraft"). Of the 10,000 people involved in such accidents since 1983, about 90 percent were not injured, and only 5 percent died. Interesting! Even though commercial flying has increased dramatically over the past decade, the percentage of accidents has actually dropped, compared to earlier-year percentages. And what do you suppose the odds are for accidents in your comfortable, seat-belted auto? Statistics-wise, about five million times greater! Better get over your acrophobia, it's obvious the skyway is a much safer environment than the highway.

ALAMO

There indeed was a famous last stand taken by a small group of determined fighters for Texan independence at the old Alamo in 1836, but not all the defenders fought to the last man, as legend has it. Although most of the 180 Americans were outgunned and died in the old church, at least one of the more prominent men—Davy Crockett—was captured and held elsewhere for a period of time, along with a handful of his associates. Later, General Antonio López de Santa Anna, after a Mexican-style colloquy with General Castrillon, had them summarily executed.

ALASKA HAS DROUGHTS?
How could a place like Alaska, with all that falling snow, permafrost, and soaking-wet polar bears, experience drought conditions? Impossible! The truth is, Alaska does have water shortages, sometimes of rather serious consequences, especially during the summer in the panhandle area. Another water-shortage area is the north's coastal plain, where, from October through May, fresh water is extremely scarce, being found only in a few lakes and in the aquifers of the biggest rivers. A conflict still exists between the fisheries industry and the oil field operators over water for camp use or drilling. Juneau's Mendenhall Valley is perched on glacial outwash where the water table is within a few inches of the surface, preventing use of shallow wells due to the risk of contamination. The problem is further exacerbated because ground conditions and intruding sea reduces fresh water wells where villages have been built.

ALCOHOL
If ever there were a good/bad chemical dichotomy, alcohol would have to be it! Unfortunately, most of the bad aspects have to do with how we use it (or abuse it!). What's more, there are endless misconceptions concerning this universal but troublesome compound. Following is a brief boozologist list of some of these alco-myths:

a. Alcohol keeps you warm. Not so! Imbibing booze in cold weather only gives the *illusion* of warmth. What it really does is rob the body of heat by causing blood vessels near the skin's surface to dilate. Don't mothball your long johns! Of course, you know that alcohol isn't a stimulant but a depressant.

b. Beer is not intoxicating. Beer lovers may think the hops they're drinking is less likely to lead to alcoholism than distilled liquors such as scotch or brandy. They should know that alcohol in a twelve-ounce can of beer is just as intoxicating as the alcohol in a five-ounce glass of wine or a one-and-a-half-ounce shot of eighty-proof liquor, and no less harmful. Ounce-for-ounce there is more alcohol in hard liquor, but because beer is consumed in much larger amounts, the overall consumption of absolute alcohol is about the same. Simply stated, booze checks out as booze, whether it be wine, beer, or spirits.

c. Alcohol is brewed only from grains and fruit. It is not generally known that alcohol can be distilled from a seemingly endless number of sources besides grains—plants, fruits, vegetables, aromatic herbs. Virtually anything that rots can produce alcohol to some extent.

d. Sloe gin is a type of gin. Sloe gin has nothing to do with slowness, nor is it even a gin, as the name signifies. It is a liqueur.

e. Alcohol costs more today. Despite the occasional grumbling by today's drinkers, it can be said, "They've never had it so good." When adjusted for inflation, alcohol is considerably cheaper today than in previous years. Federal taxes on beer and wine have not risen since 1951 (under Harry Truman). Only in 1985 did taxes increase on hard liquor—19 percent, which rise was quickly wiped out by inflation. However, current proposals to increase the "sin tax" levied against alcohol may alter the above figures.

ALCOHOL AND AMERICAN INDIANS
The frontier notion that Indians (Native Americans) went on the warpath after heavy drinking is a myth. Nor is it true that they metabolize liquor at a different rate than people of

other races. Some Indians drink, some don't. Some prefer drinking with the braves, others with the squaws; still others prefer a lonely spot—much the same as the non-Indians.

ALLIGATOR SHIRTS
Don't look now, but all those slithering reptiles logoed onto the front of summer shirts are not alligators, they are crocodiles. Look for the long slender snouts before you buy!

ALTIMETERS, ANEROID
The aneroid or barometric altimeter tells the Red Baron how high he is above sea level, but he can't expect a consistent reading from it because altimeters measure altitude only in terms of barometric pressure. Therefore any given altitude has a specific pressure that changes in accordance with the prevailing weather. That's why frontal systems moving into an area can greatly affect an altimeter's reading. A second and more accurate kind of altimeter is a radio device that determines absolute altitude above the earth's surface by measuring the time needed for radio waves to be reflected from the surface of the earth.

AMERICA
Probably no more unforgivable misinformation exists about the country in which we live than the name itself—America. Canadians become downright miffed (and rightly so) when arrogant south-of-the-border tourists declare: "We are from America!" Well, indeed! And is Canada not also in America? We gringos pull the same thing on the Mexicans, who also live on the North American continent. Perhaps South Americans have the most legitimate claim to being called Americans inasmuch as the name "America" was given to that continent before it was extended to North America. Yes, it's great to be an American! Especially if you live in Canada, the United States, Mexico, or Central America!

AMERICAN IMMIGRANTS

Emma Lazarus's famous, stirring poem concerning the pitiful plight of the immigrants who arrived in America during the late 1800s and early 1900s bleeds with pathos—"the tired and poor," the "wretched refuse of your teeming shore," etc. While it is true that some of the immigrants were penurious and destitute, it is also true, according to many accounts, including those of U.S. Senator Daniel Moynihan, that "those 'huddled masses' were actually an extraordinary, enterprising and self-sufficient people who knew exactly what they were doing, and doing it quite on their own." In fact, says he, "they weren't any more wretched than any other immigrant groups, including the Pilgrims. They deserve to be remembered not as teeming masses, unkempt, uneducated, and uncouth, but as the energetic bunch of enthusiastic go-getters that they actually proved to be."

AMERICA THE BEAUTIFUL

Many people have the understanding that the stirring patriotic song entitled "America the Beautiful" was written by Katherine Lee Bates. It wasn't! She was the lyricist. Furthermore, there have been over sixty melodies adapted to Bates's poem, the most familiar one, of course, being the tune written by S. A. Ward. Therefore, there is, in fact, no single officially accepted tune for "America the Beautiful." Also the currently familiar poem is a changed version of her original 1893 work, which she rewrote eleven years later so as to be less literary and ornate.

ANTARCTICA

Most people view Antarctica as a desolate, grim, flat, and inhospitable part of the earth where no life can be found and where few have ventured. But Antarctica has considerable topographical diversity, with mountain ranges reaching upward of 16,864 feet, notably Vinson Massif. Great rivers of ice (glaciers) grind slowly down from the valleys of those high mountains all the way to the sea. Despite having the greatest concentration of ice in the world, it also has dry-land coasts where most of the wildlife assembles. Also, most people credit the Arctic with having the earth's coldest temperatures, but Antarctica's mean temperature is decidedly colder than that of the Arctic. (The coldest weather ever recorded was at Antarctica's Bostok Station in 1960, where the temperature fell to minus 127°F.) Yet only about four to six inches of snow accumulates yearly.

ANTI-SEMITISM

To most people the term *anti-Semitism* suggests a hostility toward the Jewish people. But "anti-Semitism" is really a term of convention, and being so, it is only partially correct. Arabs and some Ethiopians are Semites, as are numerous other Mediterranean-strain people of which the Jews were once a subtype. Yet it is almost certain that those who hold anti-Semitic sentiments do not have Arabs or Ethiopians in mind. Actually it would be technically correct to use the word *Semitic* to identify any people who speak the Semite languages, yet, for religious, ethnic, and/or political reasons, the term is directed only at the Jews.

APPLES AND ALAR

The much-maligned food additive—alar—once added to apples was notorious for the wrong reason. For the record, treating apples with alar is not done primarily for cosmetic purposes, i.e., luster; it is done to keep the crunchy pippins on the tree so as to reduce crop loss and subsequent rotting. Alar is a growth regulator. As to its harmful potential, a mouse would have to devour the entire apple orchard in order for the trace elements to slug the miserable rodent. This is not to argue for or against the use of alar, but the stuff had been in use for over twenty years without a single case of apple-caused human expiration.

APPLESEED, Johnny

Although there really was a person nicknamed Johnny Appleseed, an American frontiersman who appeared along the Ohio River planting apple seeds in the interests of helping rural society, his actual name was not Johnny Appleseed but John Chapman, upon whom history has endowed legendary status. Nurseryman, herb doctor, minor military hero, he was also a religious eccentric scattering the seeds of Swedenborgian dogma to every village and town. He wasn't too pious, however, to avoid wealth, having accumulated over a thousand acres of valuable land back home.

ARISTOTLE

The mere mention of Aristotle, the Greek philosopher and scientist, evokes an image of unmatched wisdom, wit, and sagacity, but history gives the pensive sophist a far-less-impressive printout. It has been shown by scholars that despite Aristotle's enormous influence on the world's thinking, it could be argued that he was wrong far more often than he was right—so often that his ideas actually *delayed* the progress of science rather than advanced it. Roger Bacon, the great thirteenth-century friar and philosopher, once declared: "If I had my way I should burn all the books of Aristotle, for the study of them can lead to a loss of time, produce error and increase ignorance." Aristotle, you may remember, was the sage who declared that a common housefly had only four legs.

ARTHRITIS

It is often thought arthritis is a disease that affects only the bones and joints of the body. But actually there are many different arthritic-type diseases involving more than the joints and connective tissues. Rheumatoid arthritis, for instance, is really a generalized disease, not limited to bones and joints. It can also involve other tissues such as the eyes or lungs, which can be permanently damaged. For those who are inclined to think arthritis is a single disease, it should be pointed out that medical science has identified over *one hundred* different types of arthritis.

ASIAN-AMERICANS

With the troubled countries of the Orient sending over their boatloads of seeming derelicts to the teeming shores of America, there's little wonder that Asian-Americans are the fastest-growing population in the United States. This has led to the belief that this influx of Orientals has placed an unnecessary burden on North America, supposedly increasing the public dole and depriving others of opportunities. The facts, however, show just the opposite. More than one-half of adult Asian Indians, and over one-third of Chinese and Filipinos living in the United States, are college graduates. According to the 1985 report in the *Population Bulletin* edited by G. W. Gardner and B. Robey entitled "Asian-Americans: Growth, Change, and Diversity in 1980," 35 percent of the six primary Asian-American groups—Chinese, Filipinos, Japanese, Koreans, Asian Indians, and Vietnamese—had graduated from college, compared to 17 percent of Caucasian adults.

ASPIRIN

"You can't buy a stronger aspirin!" goes the old advertising slogan of a major brand-name aspirin company. And a very clever ad indeed! It gives the impression that its aspirin is somehow more effective than other brands without having to really say so. But all the other brand names can make the same claim. Why? Because aspirin sold by the major companies is a controlled product—made according to United States Pharmacopeia standards (five grains) as to quality and strength. Therefore, a lesser-advertised brand at $4.50 per hundred tablets is just as safe and effective as the heavily-advertised brands that sell at $5.00 per hundred. In other words, 500 milligrams of aspirin found in Company A's bottle are the same strength as 500 milligrams of Company B's aspirin, unless perchance one company's aspirin tablet is slightly larger. Chemically speaking, aspirin is aspirin and nothing more. The labels may show other ingredients such as coating material, taste masking, release control, and other things to make the tablets more consumer-attractive, but they are inert ingredients that do not alter the chemical makeup of the basic drug. If it were possible to obtain the basic ingredients to make aspirin (and it probably is), one could mix up a bucketful of aspirin at a fraction of the cost of Company A, B and C combined. Talk about a profit margin! Aspirin has it. The little pellets have an intrinsic value equal to a decimal followed by several zeros and a number one.

ATMOSPHERE, Earth's

It is believed by many that the gaseous atmospheric envelope surrounding our planet is made up primarily of oxygen. Don't we inhale oxygen through our nostrils? Aren't airplanes and automobiles powered by a mixture of oxygen and petroleum? Don't whales hump up out of the water to suck in a blowhole full of needed oxygen? Mostly not! That's because 78 percent of the air we breathe is nitrogen, the lesser component being oxygen. Oxygen, of course, is important biologically, but so is nitrogen; they both have a characteristic cycle of interaction with plants and animals.

ATOMS

We tend to regard atoms as specky snippets of something or other, encircled by electrons orbiting in a precise solar-system configuration. This is not so! The electrons stay in no clearly definable path; rather they circle the atom within cloudlike shells or regions.

ATONEMENT

To most Christians, the death of Jesus Christ on the cross is the only recorded act of atonement. Not so! A reconciling atonement is a recurring theme in the history of religion since the early Hebrews. The ten "days of awe" culminating in the Day of Atonement—Yom Kippur—reflects back to those early Hebrew beliefs of man's reconciliation to God.

AUTOMOBILE ACCIDENTS

Where do most of the slam-bang car crashes take place? On the lonely desert highways? amid the stop-and-go city traffic? or perhaps on the short, hurried trip to the supermarket for a carton of eggs needed for tomorrow morning's breakfast? Better pick the latter! According to the National Safety Council, the nonprofit organization that promotes accident prevention, the greatest percentage of car accidents occurs within five blocks of your own home.

AUTUMN LEAVES

It's often speculated that Jack Frost is responsible for painting all those spectacular color scenes in the fall of the year, but that isn't really Jack's job. It is the general weather conditions and rainfall that have the principal role in bringing about this magnificent autumnal color display. Colors change when chemistry changes—from the spring and summer chlorophyll-manufacturing days to the fall season when lower temperatures and reduced sunlight stop the trees' food-making process. Chlorophyll breaks down, green color disappears, pigments form, and nature's rite of passage is ushered in with splendiferous fanfare. Old Jack Frost's appearance may put a little bite in autumn's fragrant air, but he doesn't have the magic to turn the whole world from green to red.

B

BABY RUTH CANDY BAR

Coincidentally, the Baby Ruth candy bar and the famed New York Yankees baseball player Babe Ruth came on the American scene about the same time—the 1920s—but that's where the similarity ends. The delectable candy bar was not named after the legendary slugger, as has often been surmised, but after the daughter of former President Grover Cleveland, who at the time was gaining the affection of an admiring American public. However, this propitious timing did give the Babe a batter's chance for personal gain by introducing his own namesake candy bar. The Curtiss Candy Company, however, was in the other bullpen and didn't like Babe's idea one bit; it brought a nutty-sweet litigation against him in 1930 and the great Ruth struck right out of the candy business!

BACH, Johann Sebastian

The great and prolific J. S. Bach, born of seven generations of active musicians, is regarded as one of the truly gifted composers of all time (having sired twenty children, he had to be prolific), but contrary to what is generally thought, Bach was not heralded in his day for his genius as a *composer*, but for his virtuosity on the organ, along with his unmatched knowledge of that instrument. It took nearly a century for Bach to gain a reputation for his compositional talents, the major works of which were seldom performed during his lifetime. One obituary on Bach reads: "Our Bach was the greatest organ and clavier player that ever lived." Much of his music was generated from his testing of organs presented to him for opinions as to their quality. Perhaps that is where he developed that peculiar plinky-plinky style of composition that is found in much of his music.

BAGPIPES
Although bagpipes are most generally identified with the country of Scotland, they by no means originated there. Bagpipes were played in Europe in the thirteenth century and were mentioned in the ninth. Earlier but sparse evidence shows that Persians were dandy bagpipers. Latin and Greek references also mention the wind-whiny instrument.

BANANA OIL
Despite its suggestive name, banana oil is not derived from bananas. Rather, this clear liquid mixture, used mainly in fingernail polish and flavoring extracts, is made from nitrocellulose and amyl acetate. It smells somewhat like bananas, but you wouldn't want to put the stuff in your cream pies.

BANANA TREES
Two important bits of misinformation about the tropical fruit bananas (family name: Musaceae) require correcting. First, bananas do not grow on trees as is widely thought; they grown on plants—the banana plant has no woody trunk or boughs. Second, the same banana plant does not continually produce bananas, nor does it produce more than one bunch per plant. After a single bunch of bananas is picked, either the plant dies and the rotting stock returns to the ground as a natural nutrient, or more often the growers intercede and cut the dying plant in anticipation of new young plants that are produced by the roots of the mature parent plant. So remember, it's a one-shot deal with that scrumptious fruit. Talking about trees that *aren't,* bamboo trees also are not trees; they too are plants.

BANKRUPTCY
As complicated as the process may sound (and usually is), an individual does not legally need a lawyer to file for bank-

ruptcy. Whatever papers are required for the declaration may be obtained from a stationery store. If you decide to go solo with your business bust, the court is going to charge you a process filing fee, but if you're halfway astute and most of the way patient, you're going to save some bucks.

BARBER POLE

Most of us, especially the older generation, remember the familiar red-and-white-striped barber poles displayed in front of our country's many village barbershops, whirring endlessly, ever fascinating. But few people know the significance of those barber poles, regarding them only as a clever attention-getter for bringing in business. In reality, those poles date back to the days when barbers were surgeons, the striped colors representing the red blood and the white bandages with which the barber wrapped his patient after bloodletting.

BARBERSHOP MUSIC

Was the artform of barbershop music another of America's "firsts," or did this unique style of singing have its beginnings elsewhere? Barbershoppers won't want to hear this, but their beloved music is *not* indigenous to America; it dates back a tad—to the sixteenth century. One of the regular haunts of musicians in the sixteenth, seventeenth, and early eighteenth centuries was the barber's shop, where patrons awaiting their turn for shaving, haircutting, bloodletting, or tooth-drawing extemporized songs either vocally or on their instruments. In England this tradition of music-making has long been referred to as "barber's music." Cervantes in *Don Quixote* (1604) says, "Of the priest I will say nothing; but I will venture he has the point and collar of a poet, and that Master Nicholas, the barber, has them too, I make no doubt; for most of all of that faculty are players on the guitar and song makers" (Jarvis's translation, ch. 119). Apparently three centuries of barbershop music was enough even for the merry barbers of England and it ceased in the earlier part of the eighteenth century. Dr. William King (*Works,* Vol. 2, 1760) says that they took to periwig-making (i.e., added an occupation that filled their vacant time) and forgot their music. So the British dropped the custom of noisy extemporaneous music-making and wafted it over into (who knows exactly how, or when) the convivial barbershops of America. We know these barbershop guys and gals are around when we hear their whiny, chromatic melodies in concerts all over the country, and we go nuts trying to interpret their stretched-out acronym displayed on their automobile bumper stickers—SPEBSQSA—(the Society for the Preservation and Encouragement of Barber Shop Quartet Singing of America). Viva la barbershop music!

BARTON, Clara

It is often mistakenly believed that Clara Barton—the "Angel of the Battlefield" during the U.S. Civil War—was the founder of the International Red Cross. She did indeed found the American Red Cross in 1882, and was its president until 1904, but it was Swiss banker Jean-Henri Dunant who founded the first International Committee of the Red Cross in 1864. His book, *Recollections of Solferino,* became the catalyst for the arousal of interest in the plight of wounded and suffering fighting men who fought in the Battle of Solferino. Other honors and distinctions of that great humanitarian, unknown to most people, are that he founded the Young Men's Christian Association (YMCA) and was a co-recipient of the first Nobel Peace Prize in 1901. Unfortunately, he also went bankrupt due to his many personal sacrifices, and spent the rest of his life in obscurity and poverty.

BATS

Not many people are batty over bats, except perhaps Count Dracula and other such spooky specters. But if the beastly bats were better understood, most of the bat taboos would disappear. First of all, bats are not flying mice, as is thought by many people and as suggested in the Strauss operetta *Die Fledermaus,* which means "The Flying Mouse." (Gracious! Uncle Mickey would be appalled at such a comparison!) For the record, bats are classified as belonging to their own order called Chiroptera, meaning "winged hand." Another bat myth is that all bats are nocturnal. They're not! Some bats in a few remote islands insist on being birds—they fly by day and snooze by night. Bats are also picked on for being aggressive and for having bad dispositions. Again not true! One biologist even compared the gentle bats to "winged hamsters." As to their being rabid, far more raccoons, wolves, foxes, dogs, cats, and skunks carry rabies than do bats. When it comes to bats it's best to let the little creatures do their thing—ridding the earth of zillions of insects that would otherwise drive us all batty if the little vampires were to go on strike for a month or so.

BATTLE OF BUNKER HILL
America's first major battle, the Battle of Bunker Hill, took place not on Bunker Hill, but on Breed's Hill near Boston. In June 1775, in the first year of the Revolutionary War, thousands of colonists besieged the British army in Boston. British Lieutenant General Thomas Gage planned to fortify the hills on Charlestown Peninsula, across the Charles River north of Boston, after he received reinforcements from England. The Americans heard of the plan and decided to occupy Bunker Hill before the British could. On the night of June 16, American troops under command of Colonel William Prescott moved onto the peninsula. Disobeying orders from the command's headquarters, they bypassed Bunker Hill and fortified Breed's Hill because it was closer to Boston. The battle ended in a sort of stalemate, because although the Americans' losses were less than half those of the British, they ran out of ammo and had to skedaddle from their advantageous position.

BEARS BARING THEIR TEETH

Do they? Taxidermists and overly imaginative wildlife painters obviously think so. They like to show Brer Bruin standing tall and menacing, with claws extended and an open, savage mouth full of six-inch teeth. But bear experts tell us that baring teeth in such a way is not a natural mannerism for that animal even when in the attitude of attacking. Perhaps some bears do bare their teeth, but those that keep their mouths shut usually don't end up getting stuffed.

BEER CONSUMPTION

Germans have long been noted for their quality belly-beer and their prodigious thirst for the foamy ale, but, contrary to popular opinion, the beer-guzzling prize (per capita) goes to the *Belgians.*

BEETHOVEN, Ludwig van

It is a generally held belief in music circles that Ludwig van Beethoven became completely deaf halfway through his composing career. But to say he was *totally* deaf is inaccurate. His own notes bear out the fact of his *partial* deafness when he wrote: "At the theatre I must sit near to the orchestra in order to follow the action." Obviously Beethoven's hearing loss dealt a savage blow to his *spirit,* plunging him into depression, but the great "musical emancipator" wasn't finished as a composer by any means. He wrote some of his most important compositions while in that silent world, including perhaps his greatest work—the Ninth Symphony.

BELL, Alexander Graham, inventor of the telephone

Certainly, Alexander Graham Bell deserves full credit for designing a workable and commercially practical device to transmit sound, and he was the first to understand the possibility of voice transmission, but his device was only an improvement on earlier devices and concepts that transmitted sound. The essential elements necessary for the telephone were available at least a third of a century before Bell's patent was granted in March 1876. In the 1820s, English scientist Charles Wheatstone demonstrated that musical sounds could be transmitted through metallic and glass rods, although he abandoned the idea in favor of his telegraph work in the late 1830s. Later work done by German schoolteacher Johann Philipp Reis in 1861 actually produced several instruments used to transmit sound, devices which he himself called "telephones." Also, Englishman Elisha Gray understood how he might build a telephone receiver and actually constructed one in the spring of 1874.

BILLY THE KID
The lack of documentation concerning the life of the notorious Billy the Kid has pushed imaginations to the outer fringes of the ridiculous. Though a proven killer, the boyish-looking malcontent nevertheless did not do most of the gunslinger deeds attributed to him by today's pseudo-historians. On the contrary—he never robbed banks, trains, candy stores, or old ladies; he never had his name put on "most wanted" posters; nor was he the fastest gun in the West who faced off other desperadoes in the middle of boardwalk towns. Most accounts do suggest he was indeed a pimply, buck-toothed kid, probably about seventeen, whose real name was Henry McCarty.

BIRDS FEELING PAIN
Contrary to public belief, birds do not feel pain; if so, only a modicum of pain at best. According to ornithologists and other respectable birders, a requisite for feeling pain is the degree to which consciousness has been developed, and birds are considered to have little or no consciousness. (Maybe that's why seagulls hang out at garbage dumps and why the wingless dodo bird didn't make it past the seventeenth century, when it allowed itself to be mugged by the monkeys

and hogs of the Mauritius Islands.) According to the consciousness criteria, insects and reptiles would also be pain-
free.

BIRD FORMATION FLYING

It's obvious, isn't it—geese, pelicans, and other large birds fly
in a **V**-formation to allow each bird a clear field of vision
ahead, right? Well, now, right off that doesn't make sense
because a straight-line, lateral formation would also give
each bird a clear field of vision ahead. Actually, the birds
have more practical reasons for flying the **V** than just getting
a bird's-eye view. Here's what happens: When the lead bird
flaps its wings, it creates a vortex out near the wing tip, which
allows the trailing birds to take advantage of the updraft,
making it easier for the trailing bird to stay aloft, and so on
down the line. After time, the wearying lead bird drops back
in the formation and a new bird becomes the squadron
leader. A 1970 study published in *Science* magazine stated
that the range of flight can be extended by 70 percent when
birds fly the **V** formation. My only question is, how do the
heady honkers figure out which colleague first gets to lead
the formation?

BIRTHDATE OF CHRIST

Important events of history have always been used to mark
chronological time, and no event has been so heralded and
honored as the birth of Jesus Christ, which date we call A.D. 1.
But, contrary to long-standing convention, the year "one"
was not the year in which Jesus was born. Prior to the sixth
century the Western world followed the Roman calendar,
which began the year Rome was believed to have been
founded. After the sixth century, based on the calculations of
monk Dionysius Exiguus, the years were renumbered to
equate to the birth of Jesus Christ. However, according to
scholars, the circumspect monk's figures were not quite
accurate and the certain date of Christ's birth is still arguable.

We now know that Jesus was born during a census taken by crafty old King Herod, who died in 4 A.D. Estimations are that Christ was born up to three years before that date, and according to the New Catholic Encyclopedia, the most probable date was 6 or 7 B.C.

BIRTH MONTHS
It is often wrongly assumed that the winter months of January and February are the months in which more babies are born. But September actually is the busiest month of the year in the baby business—about 11,000 born each day in America. What many would guess to be the busiest month for births turns out to be the least active—January, with approximately 1,300 less births than September.

BLACK BEARS
When is a black bear not a black bear? The answer is about 20 percent of the time! Although most American black bears are indeed black, the aberration is that quite a substantial number of them are cinnamon or tan-colored or blond, even within the same litter. Another misconception about black bears is that they repair to a state of complete hibernation during the winter months. Not so! Although they neither eat, urinate, or defecate during their winter repose, they are never totally zonked out, and they even prepare their snooze caves for birthing their young.

BLACK HOLES
Even assuming there are such things as black holes out there in the big void, we don't know for certain they exist. (No one has seen a black hole, measured one, or fallen into one.) Therefore, most opinions about them are not provable. But if they do exist, we have to clear up a misconception: A black hole isn't a "no-thing"—a nondescript sucking machine—it is a "some-thing," albeit a very small some-thing. Astronomers

say they are once-gigantic stars that have imploded themselves down to a fraction of their original size, leaving them
with such incredible density that even light can't escape from
their mass. One thing is certain, however: Nobody in our
generation need worry about being vacuumed into one;
they're still shrouded in mathematical theories that require
far more substantive proof of their existence than we presently have. So, for now, they're science fiction, albeit plausible
science fiction!

BLOOD THINNERS, Anticoagulant

For people who have experienced heart attacks or strokes,
doctors routinely prescribe medicines such as Coumadin or
other trade names, ostensibly to "thin" the blood. (We can
thin paint, why not blood?) But the term *blood-thinner*,
though used regularly by the doctors themselves, is a classic
misnomer. Even after the patient takes such blood-thinners,
the viscosity of blood remains relatively constant—not significantly thinner or thicker. Essentially, what such medicines
do is control the rate of coagulation with the intent of
avoiding clots that might form in the veins and arteries of the
body. This is not to say that blood can't become soupy thin
due to other causes such as the blood platelet disorder called
polycythemia, a condition wherein the body makes too many
blood cells, which may induce undesirable clotting. But the
little pink pellets prescribed as blood thinners do not thin
blood. Then why in the name of "fat blood" do doctors
continue to use the term *blood thinners*? Probably because
they're better at prescribing than they are at educating.
Besides, providing a crash course in pharmaceutics to twenty
million patients is hopelessly nonproductive, and would only
lead to having to tell them that these so-called blood thinners
weren't intended for humans in the first place. They were
first developed as rat poison; they clobber the little varmints
quite effectively.

BLOOMERS

The undergarment worn by women in earlier days called bloomers—a garment designed surely to bring on the giggles from the young boys of that day—was not so named because of its shape or its tendency to bloom out to fit different-sized hips. The name relates to the inventor—Amelia Jenks Bloomer of New York, U.S. women's rights and temperance advocate of the mid-1850s. Bloomer's bloomers consisted of more than a single garment; they were a type of uniform she prescribed as a "rational dress for modest fashion—short jacket, extended skirt and turkish-type trousers gathered at the ankles." Ms. Bloomer apparently wanted to cover up all bare flesh except the face, hands, and possibly a toe or two.

BLUE MOON

During the last week of December 1991, people were able to observe a lunar phenomenon known as the "blue moon." Several theories exist as to the origin of the term *blue moon*, but one thing is clear—a blue moon isn't blue. Rather it has to do with the somewhat rare phenomenon wherein two full moons appear in the same month, as was the case on the above date. The Richard Rodgers and Lorenz Hart song "Blue Moon" may put you in a romantic mood, but it can't be blamed on the earth's silver satellite.

BODY TEMPERATURE

The temperature of a *healthy* body (whatever that might be) is assumed to remain at a toasty undeviating level of 98.6°F. This is not so, nor does one have to be sick to lower or raise it. Everyone has a built-in thermometer and a biological clock that keep the body in fluctuating sync as it adjusts to time and temperature. By about 5:00 or 6:00 P.M., body temperatures rise to a high of about 99.0°, and gradually drop to a low of 97.0° by about three or four o'clock in the morning. A woman's body temperature varies during the month in response to her menstrual cycle. So there's a body temperature spread of at least 2 degrees during the day for most everyone.

BONE FRACTURES

It is only logical to assume that since a simple bone fracture has only one break, a compound fracture must have more than one break. Logical, but wrong! The bare-bone fact is that a compound fracture is also a simple one-break fracture wherein the sharp point of the broken bone protrudes through the flesh, resulting in an open wound. Bones that sustain more than one break are called *multiple* fractures.

BONES OF THE BODY

Most often we assume that the number of body bones we were born with is exactly the number we retain throughout life. This is not true. The average baby is born with approximately 350 bones but during the growth years, many of our bones fuse together as one, producing an average bone total of only 205. It is also generally assumed that all bones articulate with each other (that they are attached), but the throat has a silly kind of bone called the hyoid bone, located in a receding angle between the chin and the neck, which is not in contact with any other bones of the body.

BONFIRES

To most people, especially youngsters, a bonfire is a calming, comforting experience, punctuated by fun and the crackle and smell of burning pine wood—a sort of wienie, marshmallowy fancy that warms the heart. But it wasn't a pleasant experience for those in bygone days, because such fires were fueled by the burning bones of corpses—they were fires of immolation and funeral pyres. Christians and heretics especially hated "bone-fires"!

BOOMERANG

The wooden throwing device called a boomerang is so "Aussified" that virtually everyone believes it originated in

Australia. Solid evidence reveals that it didn't. Many other countries had the boomerang, so it is difficult to determine its precise origin. We *do* know, however, that the early Egyptians were boomerangers. In the very recent excavation of a tomb at Abu Sir, Egypt (May 1993), among the artifacts found was a well-preserved boomerang, probably the property of Min-Nakht, the chief of Pharaoh Ramses II's charioteers, the overseer of his bowmen, and his personal envoy. This puts the old boomer way back to at least the time of Ramses II.

BOOTH, John Wilkes

Perhaps the biggest myth surrounding the Lincoln assassination is that the dastardly deed committed in Ford's Tenth-Street theater in Washington, D.C., April 1865, is a closed case, that there are no more clues to surface, no more questions to be asked about the actual slaying of this most loved of America's presidents. But despite the 125-year hiatus from that day to the present, the jury is still out on some of the most fundamental questions involving the famed conspiracy. The facts behind the man who fired the one-shot derringer continue to be magnified, discredited, and added to, making it most unlikely that the full and authentic story will ever be learned, or that everyone will be satisfied as to the actual facts. But after we have thoroughly villianized the man John Wilkes Booth, we must now understand who he was, or better, who he *wasn't*. History has it that Booth was a crazed, second-rate actor and social iconoclast, a loner. But actually he was a talented and accomplished thespian whose annual earnings reportedly would equate with the very highest salaries paid to present-day actors, taking into consideration the difference in respective dollar values of each period. As to his being antisocial, he had many friends, albeit those of a specious and conspiring character. It is also wrongly contended that Booth was unmarried. It turns out that he was indeed married to one Izola Darcy Booth (an actress whose stage name was Martha Mills), to whom one daughter was born—Ogarita Booth. Also, there remains much uncertainty in light of recent revelations as to whether it was actually Booth who was killed by federal troops at Garrett's barn in Virginia twelve days after Lincoln's assassination. Some evidence suggests he was never in the barn, and that a Captain James William Boyd, former Rebel agent, was the man killed; the suggestion being that Booth was never apprehended. Finally, most people's understanding of the famed assassination is limited to the one man— John Wilkes Booth. Their interest and knowledge ends with him. But Booth was only *one* of the players. A total of eight persons were apprehended—four given life sentences and four executed. The saga continues.

BOTTLED WATER

People who order that extra-pure water in the big sky-blue glass bottles are convinced they are getting the purest spring water the sacred mountains can offer. But are they? The truth is, much of it may actually be drawn from *municipal water systems*—the same H_2O that flows out of their kitchen taps. The problem is that there are no government requirements obligating bottlers to disclose the source of their water. Furthermore, such "pristine" water doesn't have to meet standards any higher than those for common culinary water. The folks in the General Accounting Office issued an opinion in 1990 to the effect that bottled waters may contain potentially harmful levels of contaminants—that the FDA "could do more to ensure the safety of bottled water." Of course, this doesn't mean the watchdog bureaucrats over at GAO really know all that much about the bugs and befoulment in those big blue bottles, but it is supposed they asked those who do.

BOULDER DAM

(Or Hoover Dam, depending on the political climate at the time). It has often been rumored that during the construction of Boulder Dam, several workers lost their lives by falling into the copiously poured concrete, where they remain entombed to this day—preserved to the envy of the best ancient Egyptian embalmers. Although numerous accidents did occur during this extraordinary engineering project, there is no proof of any worker ever being killed in such a manner. As to the amount of concrete used to build Boulder Dam, it is said that if it were all laid out as a two-lane highway, it would stretch from California to New York. Dubious perhaps, but the folks at the dam's visitors' center claim to have concrete proof that it is true. (Pun intended!)

BRAIN AND PAIN

It is often erroneously assumed that because the brain is the seat of consciousness it is also the place where pain originates. In actuality, even though the brain is supposed to be sensible, it is nevertheless *insensitive*. Even cutting into it will not result in pain. Moreover, the only elements inside the cranium that can sense pain are blood vessels and membranes adjacent to those blood vessels. Even with headaches, which certainly seem to be centered inside the old noggin, the pain comes from nerve endings in the muscles and blood vessels on the *outside* of the cranium. So the next time someone suggests that your pain is all in your head, it can more accurately be said that your pain is all out of your head.

BREAKFAST—The most important meal of the day?

The terrifying admonition that a person's first mistake of the day would be to skip breakfast dates back to what are known as the Iowa Studies of the late 1940s. Current analysis tells us there is no substantive evidence supporting the notion that early-day nutritional benefits are in any way more important than the benefits of meals taken later on. The one possible exception to the breakfast-is-important notion is where nutritional *deprivation* may be involved, wherein young people, particularly, start the day hungry, which could affect their concentration and their cognitive abilities for problem-solving. However, with the well-fed folks, there seems to be no ill effects from deferring eating until high noon.

BREAST CANCER IN MEN
Who has ever heard of a man getting breast cancer? The answer is the 900 men who were actually diagnosed as having the disease in 1989. That amounts to only a fraction of the cancer cases reported for women (140,000 during that same year), but make no mistake, breast cancer can show up in the macho males as well.

BREAST-FEEDING
For convenience's sake or sundry other reasons, American mothers, in addition to mothers in most advanced countries, can't wait to take their babes off the breast, many introducing them to Elsie's pasteurized milk within a year. But on a worldwide basis, over 60 percent of the world's children do not become weanlings until age five. Now is that bonding or isn't it?

BRITANNICA, Encyclopaedia
Despite the patent suggestiveness of its name, the Encyclopaedia Britannica, now in its fifteenth edition, is not a British publication. Though it started out as a British work, conceived by two printers, Andrew Bell and Colin Macfarquhar in Edinburgh, Scotland, the reputable publication was sold to Sears Roebuck in 1928, the store that sells all those suits, scissors, and saddles. The University of Chicago picked it up in 1943 and still owns it. (Ironically, Sears Roebuck doesn't sell encyclopedias.) A word about Britannica's re-

liability as a reference guide: Although it is considered the leading general reference work in the English language (as touted by its publishers), the encyclopedia is not without its errors—many errors. In fact, physicist Dr. Harvey Einbinder spent five years compiling the many errors he observed in Britannica and published them in a 390-page book entitled *The Myth of Britannica* (Grove Press, 1964). Einbinder found over 600 articles in one edition to be outdated and flawed. Hey, now!

BUCKING BRONCOS

It has been written (quite possibly by those who lunch with members of the Humane Society rather than with the bunkhouse cowpokes) that rodeo broncos buck not because of any inherent reflex they may have, but because of a rigging device called a flank strap that is secured tightly around the animal's flank. *What nonsense!* Most "unbroken" horses when first mounted by a rider will buck virtually every time until they become accustomed to the strange and unwanted figure on their back. In Western jargon, this is called "breaking in" a horse, or bronco busting. Today, most horses are restrained from bucking in a more subtle and gentle way by placing objects on their backs, and by the horseman gradually working up to the mount. Most of the time an unbroken horse will buck even with an empty saddle. The natural instinct of a horse is to unload anything thrown over its back, and bucking and kicking in every direction is its way of doing that. All the literature on Western lore, and the illustrations by such renowned artists as Frederic Remington, Charles Russell, and others attest to the natural instincts of unbroken horses to buck. In fairness to those who have opinions to the contrary, flank straps *are* used in rodeos to assure that bucking horses *continue* to buck for an eight-second count, but to suggest that they wouldn't buck without them is barnyard baloney!

BUCKWHEAT
If you're a buckwheat lover, you'll probably be surprised to learn that buckwheat isn't wheat at all; rather it is the seed of a bush more closely related to rhubarb.

BUFFALO, American
The so-called American buffalo, which roamed from the Appalachian mountains of the East to the Rocky Mountains of the West (approximately 60,000,000 buffaloes), is not a true buffalo. The word *buffalo* is a common name given to several kinds of large wild oxen, most of which are native to Africa and India. Zoologists point out numerous differences between the two animals, one of which is that the heavily-shouldered American bison has fourteen pairs of ribs while the true buffalo of Africa and India has only thirteen. So, in reality, those old vintage nickels you've been squirreling away in your safe-deposit box are really bison-head nickels.

BULLDOGGING
The sport of wrestling steers (or bulls) down by hand isn't of recent or frontier-American origin as most are inclined to think, but dates as far back as the early Roman era where such activity was recorded as being routine. But even when we bring bulldogging into the present day as a featured sporting event there is another misconception: The art of bulldogging cannot be credited to *white* cowboys but to a *black* cowhand named Bill Pickett, one of the greatest black cowboys who ever lived. Born December 5, 1870, in Williamson County, Texas, Pickett was the second of thirteen children born of ex-slave parents. As a rodeo hand he earned special billing and the professional nickname "Dusky Demon" for his daring bulldogging techniques. His feats were especially noteworthy inasmuch as he was a mere five feet seven inches tall and weighed only 145 pounds, about half the weight of today's hefty bullslingers. In 1971, the legendary Dusty De-

mon became the first black cowboy to be inducted into the National Rodeo Hall of Fame in Oklahoma City.

BULLDOZERS, TRACTORS, AND HORSEPOWER

Observe a heavy-duty earth-moving bulldozer at work, and you'll be astonished at the prodigious amount of earth it can move in a day. One such herculean dynamo can outwork a hundred pick-and-shovelers, no contest. But most people overrate them as to their horsepower—which is surprisingly limited. While some of the big muscle machines (those over 100,000 pounds, and capable of lifting nine cubic yards of dirt) have up to 465 gross horsepower, the smaller units are powered by engines whose horsepower isn't much greater than that of your old Chrysler. Many front-end loaders, extending to over twenty-two feet in length, are powered by a mere 170 horsepower—half the horses of racy sports cars. Of course, the big mules get by with their low-horsepower/high-work-output quotient simply because of their *gear ratio.* Bulldozers may be able to lift half a house, but it takes the clodhoppers a half day to get across town!

BULLFIGHTING

Because of the popularity of the grisly spectacle of bullfighting in Spanish-speaking countries, it is erroneously supposed that Spain is where bullfighting started. It is not! Bullfighting is a sport of *ancient* origin, dating back to at least 2000 B.C. on the island of Crete. Combats with bulls were also known to have taken place in Thessaly and Imperial Rome. Even Julius Caesar egged on a few bulls (from a safe distance, that is). It wasn't until about the year 1090 A.D. that the first organized bull festival took place, wherein Rodrigo Diaz de Vivar, "El Cid Campeador," lanced a bull in the butt from horseback. With the ever-increasing popularity of bullfighting, the so-called sport became financially profitable, and selective breeding was being engaged in by the royal houses of Spain, France, Portugal, Italy, and even the Roman Catholic Church in Spain. Another misconception about bullfighting is that bulls are attracted to the color red. Hardly! Bulls will charge a matador's cape no matter what color it is. So, hail the brave matadors if you choose, but with all the cards stacked against the bull it's hardly a fair fight at all.

BUNGEE JUMPING

Today's high-jinks bungee jocks believe their aerial fun is the latest thing in the world of sports. They should think again, because sixth-century hot-doggers were bungee jumping 1,500 years earlier in several countries of the world. The only difference was the materials used—high-tech rubber tethers versus vines hanging from tall trees. It's doubtful that any of today's bungee boys would dare duplicate jumps using such primitive and unreliable tethers.

BURNT-ALMOND FUDGE ICE CREAM

Not that this bit of trivia will likely make a sugar-cone full of difference regarding your eternal salvation, nevertheless you may find it interesting to learn that burnt-almond fudge ice cream isn't made with almonds that have been in any way burned. The almonds, of course, are heated but they are not burned. The cooked almonds added to plain chocolate ice cream, plus flavoring, is all that fills up that gallon of creamy ecstasy.

BURROS

The tenacious burro, upon which so much Western folklore is based, is not indigenous to Death Valley or the Grand Canyon, or any other part of the West, as is commonly thought. Stubborn little "Brighty" came originally from Africa, and has been a pain in the antlers of the native Bighorn ever since.

C

CALIFORNIA NOT IN NORTH AMERICA?

Everybody knows that the state of California is smack-dab inside the boundaries of the North American continent, right? Maybe that supposition isn't necessarily so—geologically speaking, that is! Scientists have long known that the world is covered by enormous tectonic plates, two of which are the North American plate and the Pacific Ocean plate, both of which are on a slow-motion collision course with each other. Because the Pacific Ocean plate extends the distance all the way to the San Andreas fault (halfway inside California), people living west of the fault are actually living on the upraised edge of the Pacific plate.

CALIFORNIA WEST OF NEVADA?

California, as everyone knows, is definitely west of the state of Nevada, or is it? If you were to run a north/south longitude line through the easternmost part of California, you would find virtually all of Nevada to be west of eastern California, plus small areas of Arizona and Montana, and half of Idaho. Reno and Carson City, Nevada's capital city, are also farther west than Los Angeles. While we're in the mood for geographical illusions, a similar overlapping can be found in the area north of the United States: Considering Canada's southernmost tip—Middle Island—twenty-seven of our states lie north of Canada to some degree. Hadn't thought of that?

CALORIES AND OBESITY

The assumption is that a calorie by any other name is still a calorie, that they all contribute to weight gain, to that forbidden word—obesity. Most people would buy that assumption, but then most people would be wrong. Although all calories are units of heat energy, this energy isn't treated in exactly the same way by the body. It is primarily the *fat* calories that cause obesity, not the protein and carbohydrate calories. When a person eats complex carbohydrates— whole-grain bread, for instance—his body has to work harder to get out the energy, and some of the calories are wasted as heat, a phenomenon termed the "thermic effect." But alas, that flavorful, lip-smacking fat we consume is a different story. With it, the body doesn't have to work as hard to get out the energy. Consequently it takes on a kind of hoarding orientation, and keeps all that exceeds what is actually required for maintenance, making the body not only a fat factory but also a fat-storage facility. Disgusting, isn't it? But who knows, maybe someday food scientists will find a way to get us to actually enjoy broccoli and zucchini!

CANARY ISLANDS
The thirteen small Canary Islands situated sixty miles off the northwest coast of Africa do not derive their name from the little tweety canary bird. Rather, ancient people who discovered the islands named them for the fierce dogs they found on them—in Latin, *Canis.* The original name for the islands was provided by the Romans and translates as *insulae canariae,* "Island of Dogs." In other words, the birds found on the islands didn't give the islands their name, the dogs did.

CAPONE, Al
The king rat of the underworld during the 1920s was undoubtedly gangster Al Capone, a surly thug whose tommy-gun gang ran most of the illegal operations in Chicago during the Depression years. He and his lawless cabal killed many rival gangsters and were implicated in the St. Valentine's Day Massacre of seven men in 1929. Yet many

people assume that he paid for his crimes with his life. He didn't. In 1931, a federal jury convicted Capone not on robbery and murder charges, but of income tax evasion, for which he served only eight years in prison, followed by his fat-city retirement in Miami, Florida, where he died.

CARCINOGENS

We all relish meals guaranteed to be free of harmful chemicals, but if we had such a meal it would have to be an empty plate. That's because all food is composed of chemicals, even toxic chemicals, which are a natural part of our food. A spud, for instance, is a complex aggregate of at least 150 different organic niceties, including arsenic, carotatoxin, tomatine, nitrate, solanine, and a host of other toxins. The bad stuff can also be found in all the "health" food you've been paying premium prices for; the concentration is minuscule, but it's there! Toxins occur not only in synthetic sources but also throughout nature. The same chemicals that are found to cause cancer in laboratory animals are also a natural part of our own healthy food supply. Morever, our natural carcinogens are in fact much more widespread and numerous than the man-made carcinogens in food, and are present in much larger amounts.

CAR-RENTAL INSURANCE

Car-rental agency people at the airports and elsewhere usually suggest that car renters pay the optional insurance fee in the event the rental car is involved in an accident. Many travelers purchase the policy, but in most cases, they probably shouldn't! If the traveler already has full coverage on his own automobile (personal-liability coverage is required to get a driver's license and a driver's license is required to rent the car), that coverage, in most instances, extends also to the rental car. Knowledge is power! Or said another way: Ignorance is not bliss; it is *expensive!*

CARROTS HELP WITH THE VISION

Probably the only certain thing that can be said about a carrot's impact on the human body is that the overeating of them will give the skin the look of a carrot. The carrot/eyesight idea no doubt came from the fact that carrots contain carotene—any of several organic compounds widely distributed as pigments in plants and animals and converted in the human liver into vitamin A. But because carotene is found in many foods, the liver storehouse is usually well stocked and needn't be replenished with megadoses of vitamin A. If one's vision is a bit unclear, a visit to a good optometrist may be all that is needed. Besides, Bugs Bunny, out in Farmer Brown's garden, doesn't eat the carrots anyway—just the luscious leaves above the ground.

CASSIDY, Butch

Wild-West legends often get ballooned into fanciful folklore by whimsical writers who get their material from other whimsicalists who get their looney lore from—who knows where? The legend of Butch Cassidy and the Sundance Kid comes to mind. Neither of them were leaders of the Wild Bunch as depicted by Hollywood. At least that's the opinion of the Western Outlaw-Lawman History Association, who tell us neither Cassidy nor Harry Alonzo Longbaugh—"The Sundance Kid"—was the leader of that infamous gang. Rather it was Harvey Logan, alias "Kid Curry," who was responsible for staging the legendary bank heists and railroad holdups. Butch, whose real name was Robert Leroy Parker, and other unruly malefactors such as Bill Carver and Ben Kilpatrick were merely saddle-bag accomplices.

CATARACTS

It is mistakenly thought that eye cataracts affect only a limited number of the population, mostly the elderly. (Either you have cataracts or you don't have cataracts!) The fact is, cataracts do not obey the "all-or-nothing" law. Virtually all adults have punk peepers to some extent. (Cataracts may even be present at birth.) The most common form of cataracts begins with the long, winding-down aging process manifested by the continuing growth of the lens with its accompanying increase in density. In past years, cataract removal was a painful and protracted sack-time experience. The good news today is that even as your cataracts are progressing, corrective surgery is generally accomplished on an outpatient basis.

CATS AFFECTIONATE?

"Nobody really owns a cat," goes the old saying. True, they have a calming effect on the lady of the house and purr with the seeming affection of a newborn baby, but tabby's ways are not our ways. They show affection only on their terms. But look at the way they rub up against your legs—that's affection, isn't it? Not at all! Old tom is the biggest con artist of the animal kingdom. Actually, your pampered parlor pussy isn't particularly interested in your trousered legs other than to play out his primitive ploy of marking territory. Your legs are his make-do substitute for an elm tree, assuring himself that his olfactory trademark has been properly advertised, making him the fat cat of the neighborhood. His leg-rubbing is a throwback to earlier times when he had to scratch out a legitimate living on his own.

CATTLE RANCHES

The great cattle ranches of the United States were as uniquely indigenous to this country as the cowpokes who worked them, as traditional as the beans and bacon served from the frontier chuck wagons—a cowhand's main staple. But were the ranches really all-American enterprises as we have come to regard them? Not entirely! Prior to the 1900s most of the cattle ranches in the United States were owned by British and Scottish syndicates who taught American ranchers how to make money on a large scale. Typical of these ranches were the million-plus-acre ranches like the Matador, the King, and the XIT ranches. After the 1900s, most of these mega-spreads were downsized into many smaller-acre properties.

CEDAR WOOD

Many items today are built of what is supposed to be cedar wood—your pretty outdoor gazebo and your aromatic cedar chest, for instance. That assumption has a problem! It isn't true. The red and white cedars grown in North America are really juniper trees. The western red cedar of Canada is actually a form of arborvitae. True cedar wood—the expensive stuff—is indigenous to the mountainous areas of the Mediterranean region and the western Himalayas, namely, the atlas, the cypress, the deodar, and the cedar of Lebanon. There are varieties of ornamentals—the Atlas and the Deodar—found in the United States, especially along the Pacific and Gulf coasts, but such wood is not used for building and construction purposes. What you have in your home may smell and look like authentic cedar, but don't bet on it!

CHICKEN EGGS

Health-conscious weight watchers are aware that the white of the egg is also the "lite" part of the egg—virtually no calories or cholesterol and little redeeming taste. Its beaten fluff graces the top of pastries and pies, and is airily whipped into endless goodie recipes. They also mistakenly believe the white of the egg is the "lightest" part of the egg as to weight. Certainly it weighs less than the yolk! It doesn't! Although the white part—the albumen—has the feel and consistency of lightness, it is nevertheless heavier than the yolk. When a freshly laid egg is placed on its end or side, the yolk is suspended slightly above the egg's center because it is lighter than the white.

CHILDREN—HALF MOTHER, HALF FATHER?

It is often assumed that offspring are essentially half mother and half father. This is not so! Any person is a combination of the entire inheritable gene pool of both parents. Therefore, the union of genes from two different persons has the capability of producing virtually endless numbers of genetically different offspring. Perfect "halfness" would produce children who would all look alike, and it is known that even identical twins are not pure clones of each other. This genetic imbalance is particularly noticeable in the facial features of children more dominantly identifiable with one parent than with the other.

CHOCOLATE AND ACNE

Because of our long-standing belief that chocolate causes acne, it is doubtful the savory delicacy will ever be exonerated. But the latest scientific studies show that those teenage zits are not caused by chocolate. Chocoholics may have other valid reasons to wean themselves off the seemingly addictive cacao bean, but they'll still need a doctor's prescription for the acne.

CHOLESTEROL

The fatty substance free-floating through the vascular plumbing of the body—cholesterol—is often thought to be found in *all* foods containing fat. This is wrong! Cholesterol is derived only from *animals* and/or animal products such as meat, milk, and cheese. Your macaroni and cheese dinner contains lots of cholesterol, but virtually all of it is from the milk and cheese, not the macaroni. Another mistaken idea concerning cholesterol is that it is located primarily in the blood—floating merrily, merrily down the stream; it is not! Only about 7 percent is found in the blood, the greater 93 percent being harbored in the tissues.

CHURCH DONATIONS

One may be tempted to equate generous church donations with good times, but such is not the case. According to the National Council of Churches, 3.3 percent of the American population made regular donations to their respective churches during the Great Depression of the late twenties and early thirties. In 1989, with personal income and earning power considerably above that of the Depression years, only 2.3 percent of the population regularly donated to their church. Conclusion? Humility inflates when fortunes fall!

CHURCHILL, Winston

Credible biographers find no justification for the notion that young Winston was a dullard throughout his elementary school years. Nor did he lose any blood, sweat, and tears in passing his academic examinations. On the contrary, Winnie was, for the most part, a competent student whose class standing was always top drawer. His own flippant, self-flagellating remarks probably contributed more to those poor-student accounts than anything else. We must remember, Sir Winston was known for his wit, including that directed at himself.

CIVET CAT

Despite its name, the civet cat is not a cat. The word *civet* refers to the musky substance released from the anal glands of that particular animal, from which many perfumes are made. Undoubtedly the secretion is perfume to other civet cats too, because that's what they use to mark their territory. This non-cat actually belongs to the Viverridae family; common tabbies belong to the Felidae family. Another cat that isn't a cat is the polecat, the smelly, once-endangered varmint that also goes by the undeserved alias of the skunk. Actually, the polecat belongs to the weasel family.

CIVIL WAR CASUALTIES

Owing to the size and scope of the two world wars in which the United States fought, there seems to be a consensus that those were the wars wherein America suffered its greatest troop losses. Such an assumption is wrong! In terms of total human casualties, more men were lost in the Civil War than in all the other U.S. wars combined. Those figures must be qualified, however, in light of net battlefield casualties. While it is true that approximately one million fighting men were killed during the great Civil War (as opposed to about 503,000 for World Wars I and II), only an estimated 204,000 of that number were actually battlefield casualties. The greater number of troops were killed by disease. At any rate, one has to wonder what was civil about the Civil War!

CLOTHING AND WARMTH

Which coats are warmest, those made from wool, cotton, or fur? We often comment on how warm a coat is, insisting that some garments are warmer than others. However, clothing by itself is neither warm nor cold. What makes it feel warm is its ability to retain the heat generated by *our own bodies.* In other words, some clothing materials, such as fur, are better body-heat traps than others. And the irony is that the best wraps happen to be the high-ticket items, like the pelts of animals, which we so unconscionably take from them.

COBALT BOMB

We sometimes run across articles alluding to the so-called cobalt bomb, which is said to be an atom bomb to which cobalt has been added. Although, in the past, such a bomb had been considered, and was technically feasible, it was never actually made. Exposing cobalt to neutrons in an atomic reactor causes it to become radioactive, giving off high-energy gamma ray radiations. A bomb so constructed was considered to be a "dirty bomb," unacceptable to any nation that might attempt to construct one. So, we have one less blockbuster to worry about!

COBB, Ty

Tyrus Raymond Cobb, nicknamed the "Georgia Peach," is still considered a superstar, but he wasn't a peach to those who knew him; he was Mr. Villain personified—even to his own teammates. But time has a way of vindicating and immortalizing sports overachievers on the merits of their records alone, so what modern-day sports fan, fueled by the spirit of American hero worship, cares that Ty Cobb was one of the most disliked jerks in all of baseball. From all reports, he was nasty, selfish, arrogant, and openly bigoted, one bent on winning no matter the cost. Davey Jones, who played in the Detroit outfield next to Cobb for seven years, described Ty Cobb as having such a rotten disposition it was hard to be his friend. Jones said he antagonized so many people, hardly anyone would speak to him, one problem being that he had no sense of humor, especially about any humor directed at him. "Too bad," said Jones. "He was one of the greatest players who ever lived, and yet he had so few friends." Jim Murphy, author of the book *Baseball's All-Time All Stars,* wrote, "He was so despised that a few of his own teammates even tipped off opposing players to what they thought were Cobb's weaknesses." Ty Cobb was said to have mellowed in his later years, but it was too late. When he died in 1961, only three men from all of major league baseball attended his funeral. Maybe it's best we just remember his stats!

COBRA SNAKES

India's mesmerizing snake charmers have been fixating king cobra snakes with their supposed narcotic music for centuries, but the music itself doesn't charm cobras, who can't hear the sounds in the first place. That's because cobras are deaf and have no ears. The only people being charmed by the fallacious fakirs are those taken in by this age-old ruse. Cobras focus on moving things, which is why the charmer is seen to be constantly swaying back and forth, aware that the cobra is only following his movements. Cobras would react similarly without all that funky flute music.

COCA-COLA

The story of how the zesty Coca-Cola drink came into being is almost legendary. What is known is that Dr. John S. Pemberton, an Atlanta pharmacist and Confederate Army veteran, mixed up a jar of his secret syrup and induced an employee in a nearby drug store to add carbonated water to it, and the famous soft-drink idea leapt into lucrative fruition. The Coca-Cola story has also been fraught with many misconceptions, however. One is that the drink was initially advertised and promoted as a kind of elixir designed to "whiten the teeth, cleanse the mouth, harden and beautify the gums, prevent formation of tartar, neutralize acidity of saliva and cure tender and bleeding gums." This is not true. The product that was supposed to do all those things was a mouthwash called De-lec-ta-lave, promoted by Asa Cander, the owner of Coca-Cola at the time. However, the original formula did boast of *some* health benefits. It was advertised as a "Delightful Summer or Winter Drink" that was "Helpful for Headache and Tired Feelings, and for Relieving Mental and Physical Exhaustion." Interestingly, prior to hitting on the "Real Thing," Dr. Pemberton had been fiddling around with other slurpee versions of Coca-Cola, such as Dr. Pemberton's French Wine of Coca, which contained substances that today would be closely controlled or prescribed—alcohol, opium, morphine, and codeine. Two other things about the Coca-Cola enterprise may come as a surprise to most people: The six-pack Coca-Cola carton (something we believe is a modern innovation) actually came into being back in 1923.

COFFEE

Americans have so long thought of the stimulating brew coffee as being indigenous to Latin America that most don't realize that it is actually of Eastern Hemisphere origin. Etymologists connect the modern word *coffee* with the name Kaffa (or Kava), named after the southwest province in Ethiopia, where the first discovery of the coffee seed is said to date back to 850 A.D. However, the earliest known species—*Coffea arabica,* the coffee shrub of Arabia—is the coffee now grown so abundantly in Latin and South America. Also generally misunderstood is the fact that the coffee bean is not really a bean at all, but a seed growing inside the cherry-red fruit of the tropical evergreen coffee shrub.

COFFEE FOR HANGOVERS

There may be some psychological benefit to drinking several cups of java to sober up as some are apt to do, but that's the only benefit; nothing in the tasty drink contributes in any way to mitigating the dreaded hangover. Consuming lots of water is actually more effective, but perhaps the only dependable relief comes from sympathy and the passing of time.

COLD-BLOODED ANIMALS

All animals except mammals and birds are said to be cold-blooded, but contrary to what is often thought, such a name has nothing to do with chilled blood. The so-called cold-blooded creatures such as fish, amphibians, reptiles, or any of the invertebrates are known as poikilothermic animals because they lack the ability to maintain a constant internal body temperature. In other words, they do not have built-in thermostats. Man, on the other hand, is said to be homoiothermic, or warm-blooded, but his blood measures about the same temperature as that of poikilothermics. So we have to regard the whole idea as a cold-blooded misconception!

COLD GERMS

Most people are now aware that colds are not caused by *being* cold, but are still of the opinion that colds are caused by germs. We wash our hands to get rid of germs, we avoid cranky people with red noses and watery eyes (who we know are simply saturated with germs), and we turn our heads to escape the spray blast of an uncontrolled, germ-laden sneeze. But *germs* do not cause colds, *viruses* do—over 150 different kinds, with no effective vaccines or antibiotics available to clobber them.

COLD WEATHER AND CALORIES

It's a mistake to assume that people require increased calories during cold weather. Research shows that cold weather has no substantial effect on the body's ability to maintain a proper level of heat. Therefore, an increased intake of calories will do nothing to influence one's automatic temperature-regulating process. What matters is the amount of clothing worn to allow us to maintain a satisfactory miniclimate. Red long johns are more likely to change our thermostats when there's a change in the thermometer. (White long johns will also do the job!)

COLORADO RIVER

Your history books and encyclopedias relating to western rivers tell us that the mighty Colorado River has its source in the upper part of the state of Colorado, merges with the Green River in Utah, plows through the Grand Canyon, and finally flows over the border into Mexico to the Gulf of California, or what is otherwise called the Sea of Cortés. But the tail end of the Colorado River journey doesn't happen that way anymore. Because of the present use and abuse of the mighty river, its final demise takes place in the dry wastelands of Mexico, many miles short of the Gulf of California. No other river has been so argued over and prostituted as the Colorado, being siphoned off by viaducts, tapped by thirsty croplands and gluttonous industry, and polluted and recycled three times over in its 1,440-mile meander to its ignominious, man-caused sink into the Mexican sand. Also, most people aren't aware that two other rivers bear that same name—one originating in West Texas and flowing into the Matagorda Bay, an inlet of the Gulf of Mexico, and the other in south central Argentina, emptying finally into the Atlantic Ocean.

COLOR BLINDNESS

It is a mistake to assume that color-blind people are not able to see color. Color-defective persons see color nearly as well as those with perfect color vision. This ocular defect simply refers to the inability of persons to tell all the colors apart; their wavelength discrimination faculties are not as acute as those of the majority of people. Thus, they see many colors as identical where most people see them as different. Only a very few people are unable to see *any* color. Such people have what is called achromatic vision, being able to discriminate only shades of gray, white, and black. They would also see little point in visiting New England for the autumnal colorfest.

COLOR WHITE

It is often, but wrongly, assumed that white is the *absence* of color and that black is the *presence* of color. Actually, mixing all the colors of light gives you white, but white contains *more* than the colors of light. Conversely, mixing all the colors of pigment gives you black, but black contains more than the colors of pigment. If this one doesn't give you a blackout, try a whiteout!

COLTS

Contrary to what is generally believed, all one-year-old horses are not *colts,* only about half of them are. The other half are fillies. Putting it in human terms, colts are boys, fillies are girls. If you're still confused, take a closer look!

COLUMBUS, Christopher—Myths

If the man whom we refer to as Christopher Columbus were addressed by that particular name in his day, he wouldn't have responded. That's because it really *wasn't* his name. Historians tell us that Columbus took residency in at least three countries, where he changed his name each time to fit the local culture—Cristoforo Colombo in Italy, Cristovao Colom in Portugal, where he lived as a young man, and Cristóbal Colón in Spain, where he spent his most productive years and where he eventually died. It was the English historians who bestowed upon him his latinized name of Christopher Columbus. It's not even certain that he was Italian, despite his will, which attests to his being born in Genoa. Numerous Columbus buffs have labeled him as Portuguese, Greek, Jewish, Spanish, even Norwegian. And the most prevalent myth of all about the celebrated mariner what that he discovered America. Actually, he never set foot on the North American continent—not to mention the fact that countless millions of Native Americans had lived there for centuries before 1492, and even *they* don't claim to have discovered it.

COMMON COLD

The winter has arrived and with it the wretched, runny snouts that turn saints into sinners. But despite the obvious increase in cold-catching during the wintertime, the weather is not the direct culprit, as most people suppose, it is only a facilitator. During cold weather the schools are in session and children spend more time indoors together, thus exposing themselves to more cold viruses, and in turn exposing other family members as well. As to how the infective agents get into our bodies to give us our colds, the *hands* have been identified as being most culpable.

COMMUNICATION, VERBAL

Language experts tell us we don't really communicate the way we think we do. Whether we are aware of it or not, only a small part of our interpersonal communication is *verbal*—from 3 to 20 percent, depending on whose material you're reading. The rest is accomplished through body language—gestures, posture, facial expressions, tone of voice, even breathing. (We all know how much stressful communication there is in the "silent treatment.") These nonverbal "silent persuaders" are also the language employed by moon-eyed lovers on park benches; though the pipes are quiet, the vibes are at play and the messages get through with amazing accuracy.

CONDOMINIUM

Prior to World War II, the word *condominium* was not a general-use term; only an esoteric few would have known its meaning. Most people still suppose it to be a modern-day term, having to do with a particular type of housing. (The term *condominium* means "together" and "domain.") Today, literally millions of people live in condominiums, and don't really care about name origin, but in earlier years the word referred most generally to joint rule or ownership of a territory (an example being the joint ownership of Samoa by Germany and the United States prior to World War II). Condominium construction may be a modern phenomenon, but the word itself is old, old, old!

CONSPIRACY

It is often thought that punishment is meted out for conspiracy only when an actual crime has been *committed*, but the law takes it one step further. Even the *planning* of an illegal, treacherous, or evil act may be in itself a punishable crime regardless of whether such a crime has actually taken place.

CONTINENTS
In case you were blowing spitballs when you should have been listening to your grade-school geography teacher, you will remember that the curriculum showed the world had seven continents—Asia, Africa, North America, South America, Europe, Antarctica, and Australia. But there has never actually been an absolute consensus regarding the exact number of these large land masses. Some reference books take issue with that standard number—Europe is not a true continent, but merely a large peninsula of Asia. It is also arguable whether Antarctica meets the criteria for inclusion into the true-continent category; there probably will always be a continental question mark on the matter.

COPYRIGHTS
Contrary to public belief, it is not against copyright laws for authors to duplicate published titles. Occasionally we see title duplications and we wonder if copyright laws have been broken. But book titles have no such privilege because titles are not considered intellectual property. Copyright protection applies only to the extent of a writer's expression, not his selected title, ideas, concepts, names, short phrases, general themes, or familiar symbols. Copying ideas and/or thoughts is regarded as research. The same holds for Mr. Webster and the dictionaries named after him; his name is reusable. (Ironically, the original dictionary put out by Noah Webster did not contain his name. It was entitled "An American Dictionary of the English Language.") Finally, contrary to common thought, the Copyright Office does not bestow copyright protection, it only registers the claims to copyright. Any and all disputes become a matter of judicial concern.

COTTON GIN
Everyone knows that shrewd old Eli Whitney invented the cotton gin; everyone except our picky historians. They know Whitney invented what was probably the first *American*

cotton gin, used only for processing *American* cotton, but the first known, albeit crude, device was of Asian origin. That gin was improved on in Santo Domingo many years before Eli's idea. Look to the Asians for having developed some semblance of almost everything—they had ten thousand years to ponder the things of the earth.

COUNTERFEITING

It is universally thought that any unauthorized production of coin money is an act of counterfeiting. Technically, this is not so. Only those coins illegally produced from metal of *less* value than the original coins are considered to be counterfeit coins. Though still a criminal act, the unauthorized production of coins of the *same* metallic value is considered to be *"duplication."* At any rate, those who choose to help the Fed with its printing and coinage work often end up doing perfectly legal duplication work in license-plate production at their state penitentiaries.

COWBOY SONGS

Under the stars, next to old paint, the cowboy sings his wistful songs of the Golden West; songs like "Oh, Bury Me Not on the Lone Prairie," "Red River Valley," and "Streets of Laredo"—right out of the Old West! Not at all! These songs, and numerous others, weren't born on the lone prairie or worked into harmonica melodies by old-time cowpokes sitting around the campfire, but were originally authentic folk songs of other cultures in other countries. "Streets of Laredo," for instance, comes from (of all places) the musical traditions of Ireland, the narrative reflecting the anguish of a dying British soldier. "Red River Valley" is based on James Kerrigan's "In the Bright Mohawk Valley," which in turn comes from a traditional Canadian folk song concerning the Red River of Lake Winnipeg, Manitoba, Canada. "Oh, Bury Me Not on the Lone Prairie" was originally a poem—"The Ocean Burial," written by E. H. Chapin in 1849, and set to music by George N. Allen. The dolorous cowboy song "Wagon Wheels" didn't originate in Dodge City or Cheyenne, but in New York City. The melody comes from Antonin Dvořák's 1893 *New World* symphony, op. 95—the largo movement.

CREDIT CARDS

It appears that the plastic economy is with us for good and our compelling credit cards continue to mug us like Piccadilly pickpockets. But notwithstanding the many unsolicited credit cards that are sent via the U.S. mail to the American consumer (with names conveniently and conspicuously added), credit cards, by law, can be issued only to those who *request* them. Which means there's a loophole as big as a wind tunnel there somewhere! Renewal cards, of course, can be issued without such request.

CRIME AND UNEMPLOYMENT

Logic would dictate that a high unemployment rate would correspond to a high crime rate, particularly in the case of robbery. At least that's how the crime manual reads. But contrary to such reports, this supposed correlation has not generally been the case. For whatever tempting reasons people snitch each other's property, it apparently isn't due to the scarcity of job opportunities. For instance, relative to the U.S. population, the number of jailed persons in 1978 was 98 persons per 100,000. In 1932 (during the depressing Depression) the number of jailed persons was a mere 33 persons per 100,000, about three times short of the 1987 rate. Apparently it is a high *employment* rate that parallels a high crime rate.

CROCKER, Betty

Many people might wonder why they've never met Betty Crocker, General Mills' lady with the familiar homemaker's persona. The reason? She doesn't exist, she was born in a cake mix—a recipe of the imagination! Betty Crocker is the culmination of a series of bits and pieces of personality the company, over the years, has compounded to make into a real-person advertising logo. Her handwriting was that of a company worker—Florence Lindeberg; her expertise in baking came from numerous company employees; and her first voice belonged to one Blanche Ingersoll. Betty's first portrait was painted in 1936 by Neysa M. McMein in a style befitting a lady of charm, friendliness, and kitchen competence. Since her mythical birth in 1921, Betty Crocker has had several facelifts and will undoubtedly continue to be nurtured with all the refinements each generation of housewives will expect of her.

CROWS NOT ALWAYS BLACK

If Edgar Allan Poe had written about a red crow in his raven poem, it probably wouldn't have been published. That's because all crows (or ravens for that matter) are supposed to be black. But they aren't! Flitting about in the forests of Guyana and eastern Brazil, the largest bird of the crow family can be found—the crimson fruit crow, alias *Haematoderus militaris*. That old caw-caw crow is bright red. His militant name (*militaris*) and the fact that he is forty-six centimeters (eighteen inches) long suggest that the Brazilian big bird must be very cantankerous, and indeed he is!

CRUDE OIL

Few people have ever seen crude oil as it comes from the bowels of the earth and enters the complicated refining process; interestingly, it is not always *black*, as is mistakenly believed. Crude oil was once popularly referred to as *"black gold."* Actually, crude oil is a rainbow of colors—a mixture of thousands of different hydrocarbons, with each oil having its own mixture, which varies widely from one field to the next. Some mixtures may be brown, amber, green, or almost colorless, depending on the particular hydrocarbon makeup found in the underground pool.

CRUSADES

The long litany of hype found in historical accounts and novels about what the Crusades were all about runs the full gamut from fact to absurdity. The conventional picture framed in the minds of most people about the Crusades is that they were consecrated struggles fought by an army of highly dedicated and devout Christians pitted against an equally cause-oriented populace of Moslems, brutalizing each other for the sake of protecting and preserving their venerated dogmas. But actually, the Crusades, which spanned a period of about 154 years (1095 to 1294), were no more religious wars than political, social, or economic wars, with the spoils always going to the conqueror. The following few of many misconceptions are noteworthy:

a. The knights? Gallant perhaps, but not so Camelot-pure and noble as Hollywood would script them. Though much given to ceremony and rituals, involving themselves in traditional festivals and fasts, always receiving the daily mass, and above all, paying homage to the demanding strictures and power of the Church, many of those twelfth-century knights were murderous, superstitious, and adulterous brigands.

b. The Church? Eyes were not as singled to the figure on the cross as they were to the mystique of the cross. For the crusaders, the actual practice of Christianity came to be a much neglected stewardship. The motivation underlying the bungling Crusades was ostensibly an attempt to sustain the Christian ethic and beleaguer the infidel, but much of it was done in the spirit of pursuing political and materialistic ends. Sullied by cruelty, greed, and blind self-righteousness on the part of the Church, the so-called Holy War was little more than a long act of intolerance in the name of God, crippling dangerous monarchs, and obfuscating heretical sects, each Crusade instigated by the whims of the power-seeking papacy.

c. The peasant hordes? Not so well-intentioned and aware of what the whole charade was about as some accounts would picture, but rather a befuddled potpourri of fanatics, hornswaggled into doing the wrong thing for the supposed right reason. At the forefront of the grand melee (behind the knights and the noblemen) the Crusaders were largely a veritable rabble of aimless peasants, singing pagan songs, indiscriminately mutilating the citizenry (young and old), raping and beheading women, laying unmerciful siege to villages and towns, and slaughtering souls with Church-sanctioned impunity. Of the Crusaders, author Henry Treece tells us that for most of the hordes, Christ was but another leader among many, the Sepulchre but another stage on an endless journey toward a vague fulfillment. "Many thousands," said he, "took the cross hardly knowing that it signified anything more spiritual than that their past sins would be forgiven them as long as they kept on the move."

d. The Children's Crusade? It is often thought that the last Crusade was the Children's Crusade, but this pathetic attempt at beating the infidel was more like the median Crusade. It was preceded by four engagements with another four to follow. Actually, history is a bit fuzzy on the latter Crusades; some have been determined to have lasted beyond the usually accepted dates of termination. There is, however, general consensus when it comes to the formation and makeup of the Children's Crusade—nearly 30,000 French and 20,000 German children were killed, shipwrecked, or sold into slavery, and all under the knowing eye of Pope Innocent, who doubtlessly could have easily interdicted the whole ill-fated movement in light of the influence the Church had over the young zealots of that day.

CUBISM

The painting genre of cubism, developed in France in the early 1900s, is mistakenly regarded as an art form employing only cubical shapes. Actually, this particular movement, led by Pablo Picasso and Georges Braque, put emphasis on a broader effect—the utilization of spheres, cylinders, and cones, including the dimension of time. Some paintings such as Picasso's *Les Demoiselles d'Avignon*, of 1907, are void of any evidence of cubical shapes. Speaking of the inscrutable Picasso, it may surprise people to learn that he didn't always paint in the eccentric style that so often characterizes modern art, but was quite conventional in his work until the beginning of the cubist movement.

CULTURE

We often hear of people who are said to be "cultured," as opposed to those who are not cultured. The error in such a statement is simply this: *All* people have a culture peculiar to themselves—African tribes, for instance. If we are talking about refinement, urbanity, dignity, and the like, that is quite another question. But technically speaking, *everyone* is a cultured person, which should improve the esteem of all of us.

D

DANGEROUS YEARS

Despite the accident-prone years of our childhood lives, the reckless daredevil years of youth, and the graying years of brittle bones and clumsiness, the most hazardous year of life has been found to be the very *first year* of life. People don't get into the next danger zone of "wreck-reation" until about age sixty-five, where the odds again begin to multiply.

DARWIN, Charles

To suggest that Charles Darwin was not the first to introduce the theory of evolution and natural selection would be like suggesting that Abraham Lincoln was never President of the United States. But why history has tended to pigeonhole the truth about the important contribution of another figure— Alfred Wallace—to the natural selection theory is not fully understood. In truth, Wallace, an English naturalist, worked out a statement of evolution similar to Darwin's shortly before Darwin's own book on evolution was published. Furthermore, both Wallace and Darwin presented a joint paper announcing the theory before the Linnaean Society on July 1, 1858. It would be an exercise in futility to attempt to prove definitively which of the two hit the tape first; the unfortunate thing is that history has given all five stars to Darwin and the scraps to Wallace. Moreover, the contribution of another Darwin contemporary, Gregor Mendel, divides up the evolutionary pie even further. It was Mendel who showed how differences in plants were transmitted across the generations through the discrete particles that would someday be called genes.

DEATH VALLEY

Misinformation abounds concerning southeastern California's Death Valley—one of the hottest places on earth. (The old-timers there say the jackrabbits have to carry thermos bottles to avoid dehydration.) Because of its macabre name, few people would be inclined to put the desolate desert on their vacation agenda, but actually, Death Valley has much to offer. Its mild winters bring visitors from all over the country and far more people live there permanently than is generally thought. Unknown to most fair-weather folks is the fact that

Death Valley is a national monument, managed by the National Park Service, that it is more than 140 miles long (stretching over into the state of Nevada), that its elevation ranges from 282 feet below sea level to mountaintops rising 11,045 feet above sea level (the state's lowest and highest elevations), and that although temperatures can reach 135°F; the valley is habitat to over fifty different kinds of mammals in addition to many birds and reptiles. Rocky Mountain bighorn sheep live in the high elevations of Death Valley, and the familiar burro finds the treacherous heat to its liking. And despite its name, few people have ever died from the heat in Death Valley.

DECLARATION OF INDEPENDENCE

It's not known why so many paintings depict the Founding Fathers as a geriatric quorum of white-haired patriots. John Trumbull's famous work, *The Declaration of Independence*, is an example. The fifty-five signers of our nation's birth certificate weren't youngsters by any means, but neither were they over the hill. Discounting Stephen Hopkins and Benjamin Franklin, who were both seventy, the average age of the signers was a mere forty-three. South Carolina's Edward Rutledge and Thomas Lynch were just twenty-six and twenty-seven respectfully, and seventeen others were in their thirties, including the document's author, the brilliant Thomas Jefferson, who was but thirty-three. Hardly a body of golden oldies!

DEERFLY

We often hear of the incredibly swift speed of the deerfly (snipe fly, genus *Chrysops*), one report clocking the winged bullet at close to supersonic speed. This is Doppler-effect balderdash; the deerfly tops out at about sixty miles per hour, and even that's giving the little snipe the benefit of the doubt. Common sense would dictate that the wings of any insect propelled through the air at such a phenomenal speed would be ripped off the fly's body.

DENTAL DEBUNKS

Much misinformation exists in regard to dentistry. The following true-false entries relating to dentistry bear this out:

a. Cavities. Cavities generally do not develop in older persons, but are a teenage problem. False! Sweet-tooth elders are equally susceptible to cavities if they don't know how to use a toothbrush properly.

b. Tooth loss. The leading cause for tooth loss is cavities. False! Actually, gum disease is the main culprit, especially with older people. Dentists say flossing between the fangs really helps.

c. Toothbrushes. The best place to keep your toothbrush is in the bathroom. False! The American Dental Association recommends storing your toothbrush in the driest room in the house. Bathrooms, with their high rate of humidity, are havens for infectious disease. Another misconception has to do with how long to keep a toothbrush. Most people toss them away only after they become soft and lose bristles. Bad business! Toothbrushes are germ collectors from which diseases of everything from gum problems to bronchitis to upset stomachs can be transmitted. According to the experts it's best to chuck the old brush every two weeks or less.

d. Fluoride and tooth decay. Only young persons need to use fluoride toothpaste. False! The American Dental Association and most others in the health science fields are generally in agreement that fluoride really does reduce tooth decay. But most of the promotional action for fluoride has been aimed at young people. Actually, all people, regardless of age, never outgrow their need for some kind of cavity-prevention substance—flouride, for instance. So, Pops, maybe that baking soda isn't doing the job after all.

DICTIONARY

To a lot of people, thumbing through a dictionary is like appealing to the highest tribunal of the world of words. But dictionaries don't dictate to *people, people* dictate to dictionaries. Words are like families. They are born, get married, and have children; they become perverted, exalted, loved, and hated. Strong words survive, weak ones die. Many new words come into our bulging lexicon every year. And despite the objections of our word purists, words find their way into the dictionary because of their *drawing power*. If enough people increasingly use a certain word, it becomes accepted into the household of language. When it comes to the dictionary, man himself giveth and taketh away; the dictionary's words are by no means sacrosanct.

DINOSAURS

What strange compulsion is fueling the renaissance of dinosaur interest today is hard to say, but "dinomania" is definitely in—Old Tyrannosaurus Rex is doing OK at the cash registers almost everywhere, especially in the toy department. And with new information coming in all the time from new dino digs, there will never be a shortage of misconceptions about the big landlubbers. One false perception is that all dinosaurs were large or super large. The fact is, according to paleontologists, they ranged in size from ninety-ton colossals such as Supersaurus (140 feet long) to mites no bigger than a shrew. The smallest dinosaur known is the Mussaurus, whose length equals two automobile ignition keys and who weighed in at less than an ounce. Also, all dinosaurs were not brutish killing machines like Allosaurus and his ilk; most were vegetarians. Another false notion held, especially by Americans, is that dinosaurs were primarily confined to the western parts of the United States, where so many spectacular finds have been made. (A find, amounting to 2,000 dinosaur footprints per acre, has recently been made in the Arches National Park area.) But the fact is, dinosaurs were present on all parts of the globe in their day, even in what are now Great Britain and New York, and on many small islands. The consensus of researchers is that between 64,000 and 80,000 different species of dinos could have roamed our planet. A final misconception has to do with their demise. It is true that dinosaurs died out about 66 million years ago, but what isn't generally known is that dinosaurs went through three distinct earlier extinctions, and came close to surviving the last one. The first occurred about 185 million years ago, the second about 145 million years ago, and the penultimate one approximately 95 million years ago.

DISEASES

It is generally believed that grave diseases have complex causes and are more difficult to cure, while mild diseases have simple causes and are thus easier to cure. Though the common cold is a transitory ailment, and sounds innocuous, it is anything but a simple-cause disease, owing to the dozens of "rhinoviruses" that cause it and that result in varying manifestations of body reaction. Nor does it have a cure. This so-called simple disease cannot be arrested by antibiotics, but only by the mobilization of our own body's natural immunological defenses. Bacterial diseases, on the other hand, can often respond to penicillin and sulfonamide drugs. Furthermore, cancer, for instance, is regarded as one of mankind's dreadful diseases, yet most of the known causes are quite simple: toxic chemicals, cigarette smoking, hydrocarbon tars, the ozone problem, asbestos—all environmentally caused, generally understood, and within our capabilities to control.

"DIXIE"

Virtually everyone who has heard or hummed the stirring song "Dixie" ("I Wish I Was in the Land of Dixie") believes it to be of southern origin. It is not! Although the Confederates adopted this popular song of the Civil War period as their own unofficial national anthem, it was composed by a northerner—Daniel D. Emmett, in New York City in 1859. Emmett, a talented black musician, was born and died in Mount Vernon, Ohio. His song was originally written as a "walk-around" for the closing number of minstrel shows, at Bryant's Theatre, wherein the entire company would parade. Several sets of words, both northern and southern, were written for the song, but it has survived in the version with Emmett's original words. When Abraham Lincoln ran for the presidency in 1860, "Dixie" was used as a campaign song against him. Five years later, after the Civil War, he requested a band play it at the White House. Oh yes, but it still has that southern sound, doesn't it?

DOCK

The word *dock* is almost universally (but incorrectly) applied to the physical *structure* that facilitates the loading and unloading of ships. But a dock is not the material structure aside the ship, rather it is the *water area* in which the ship is floating. The man-made facility from which cargo and personnel are loaded and unloaded is actually the *wharf* or *pier*. A wet dock is no exception. It refers only to the water, not the wharf that borders the water. So the next time you hear about someone walking on the dock, he most likely is treading water.

DOCTORS TREATING THEIR OWN FAMILIES

It is often falsely stated that laws prevent doctors from operating on or providing treatment for members of their own family. There are no such prohibitions! In fact, in most instances, the in-house practice is in the best interests of the family. With some doctors, however, that doesn't work. Perhaps it has something to do with the biblical adage that a prophet is not without honor except in his own household. (Or words to that effect!)

DRAFT

It is mistakenly thought by most people that the military "draft" pertains only to the conscription of able-bodied persons for active duty into one of the *fighting components* of military service. However, if the need arises, the country can draft people for civilian work or for such activities as civil defense and the home guard. Drafting these noncombat people amounts to about 20 percent of the total draft. Certain persons with mining skills, for instance, were actually discharged from military service during World War II and assigned to work in the mines to assure an adequate supply of minerals for the war effort. Apparently there are other ways to get the shaft in the draft.

DREAMS

All of us have undoubtedly talked to people who claim they do not have nighttime dreams (or daytime dreams for that matter). But according to the slumber experts, with very few exceptions, those claims cannot be substantiated. Virtually all people dream; it's just a matter of *remembering* them. Much depends on the time of night when the dreams take place. If you're an early dreamer, you are apt to forget the dream, but if the coach puts you in the dream game in the fourth quarter, you'll most likely remember what you just dreamed about. So, it's generally the *time* of the dream that determines whether some people score at night or not!

DRUGS

The twentieth century ushered in the devastating drug scene, which continues to have an effect on all of society. But it's wrong to suppose that in earlier times there were better controls, and hence less drug use. Prior to the turn of the century, and before the enactment of the first Food and Drug Acts in the United States, we had no controls in place for the use of some of our most harmful drugs. In addition to the cocaine put into cola drinks, brandy was common in children's tonic, morphine was available in many places without a prescription, and a new powder pick-me-up was being sold over the counter by an aspirin company—heroin.

DRY CLEANING

If you think that ketchup-stained Botany 500 suit you just sent to the dry cleaners has actually been dry cleaned, think again. After being checked for obvious dirty spots, the suit gets slam-dunked into a vat of chemical cleaning fluids, after which the soggy garment then meets the fun-house whirl of a rapidly spinning centrifuge. The suit is then sentenced to time in a dizzying tumbler where warm air is blown through the material to dry it off prior to pressing. Not all cleaning companies have identical equipment for doing their dry cleaning, but regardless of the equipment, your suit gets unmistakably soaked in the dry-cleaning process.

DUTCH OVENS

Although no one seems to know just how the Dutch oven got its name, we know it didn't come from Holland. There is no evidence to show that Dutch-oven-style cooking had its origin in the Netherlands.

DYNAMITE

In the mid-nineteenth century, Swedish physicist Alfred Nobel invented a substance called dynamite, one of the most used of all explosives. If a person were to drop a stick of dynamite or even a full box of the explosive from a tall building, would it explode? Most people think it would. But not to fear—there would be no explosion! That's because dynamite requires a detonator for the explosion—a small metal or plastic capsule that contains an easily explodable charge. Dynamite is a designer product—over two hundred kinds of dynamite have been created since its inception, each suited to some particular type of blasting. Alfred Nobel received big bucks for his potent tamale, but later became depressed knowing it was also being used destructively in ways that caused human suffering.

E

EARDRUM DAMAGE
Popular belief notwithstanding, it isn't possible to rupture the eardrum by blowing one's nose too hard. The sensations we feel in our ears while blowing are due to vibrations resulting from pressure changes. However, this is not to recommend loud nose-honking, because other dangers may be just as serious. Also, those suffering from upper respiratory infections, with accompanying nasal discharge, should know that excessive schnozzling can send bacteria skittering from the nose to the ears and contribute to ear infections.

EARTH EXPLORATION
Despite man's innate propensity for exploring, it is a gross misconception to believe that most of our geographical hinterlands and bodies of water have been explored. A large part (indeed the greater part) of our own planet still remains unexplored. For instance, we have 6 million square miles of the Antarctic that have only been sketchily surveyed. In the interests of safe shipping and navigation, much of our dangerous rocky shelf areas of the ocean have long since been charted, but we remain abysmally ignorant concerning the topography of the vast areas of our really *deep* oceans, including the plant and animal life that exists there.

EARTHQUAKES

Every major earthquake is followed by numerous street-corner Jeremiahs with their apocalyptic pronouncements that the world's final days are imminent. Their monitions would be heeded even less if people were aware of the many life-threatening earthquakes we really have each year, most of which are unreported. The media report on perhaps a dozen or so each year—the heavyweight Richter-scale seven-pointers—but the National Earthquake Information Center records tell a more realistic story. Actually, about 6,000 earthquakes happen in the world every year, strong enough to be felt—4.0 to 4.9 on the Richter scale. These quakes are far exceeded by the enormous number of smaller seismic hiccups that show up only as miniature amplitude lines on graph paper. Although calm usually prevails during earth's daily spin, it is still a very unstable globe we live on. The following outline is descriptive of what happens each year in the grumble recesses of planet Earth:

Earthquake Magnitude and Annual Frequency

Description	Magnitude	Annual Frequency
Great	8.0	1.1
Major	7.0–7.9	18.0
Large (destructive)	6.0–6.9	120.0
Moderate (damaging)	5.0–5.9	1,000.0
Minor (damage slight)	4.0–4.9	6,000.0
Generally felt	3.0–3.9	49,000.0
Potentially perceptible	2.0–2.9	300,000.0
Microearthquakes (Measurable only with instruments)	–2.0	600,000.0

EARTHQUAKE EPICENTER

When earthquakes are felt it shakes everybody's epicenter for miles around. But there's a misconception regarding exactly where the epicenter is. Most suppose it is the precise point deep inside the earth where the seismic rupture takes place. But that is not the epicenter, it is the "focus" point. The epicenter is the point on the earth's surface directly *over* the spot where the rupture takes place.

EGOIST/EGOTIST

These two egocentric-type words are misused far more often than they are properly used. *Egoism* refers to a person's *self-interest; egotism* has to do with one's *self-worth.* Therefore, an egoist may be preoccupied with his (or her) own interests and still not be considered egotistical. Conversely, an egotist may be a boastful, unambitious clod and not be considered egoistical. Freud went bonkers figuring out the difference, so be not discouraged if the two terms still bother you.

EGYPTIAN PYRAMIDS

It is not true that all those colossal funerary rock piles built to enshrine the mummified pharaohs of ancient Egypt were built by slave labor, as is universally supposed. Rather, the pyramids were built by paid workers who took pride in selectively stacking those two-ton blocks on up to their capstone apexes. Many of the workers (probably the higher-paid honchos) were buried in tombs near their masters. A discovery of such pyramid-shaped tombs (containing ten workers) was recently made near the three great pyramids of Giza, near Cairo. At any rate, the bulk of the pyramid workers were farmers working a second job (for food and clothing) during the rainy months when farming wasn't possible. As a point of interest, one tomb contained a skull of a worker who had undergone brain-tumor surgery. It isn't known whether the poor fellow died of the tumor or of the surgical procedure; the important thing is we're talking about brain surgery accomplished some 4,600 years ago!

EINSTEIN, Albert—A Slow Learner and Poor Student?

It has often been written that the introspective Albert Einstein rang the dumbbell back in his early grades and was pathetically low on the percentile chart in virtually every subject. This makes for interesting reading and may placate underachievers, but such characterizations of the little genius are probably far from true. At least that's the view of eminent scientist Abraham Pais, who worked with Einstein during the postwar years. In his book *Subtle Is the Lord* (Oxford University Press, 1982), Pais contends: "At about age six Einstein entered public school and did very well. In August 1886, Pauline wrote to her mother: 'Yesterday Albert received his grades, he was again number one, his report card was brilliant.'...The infant who at first was slow to speak... becomes number one at school (the widespread belief that he was a poor pupil is unfounded)..." Also, a *New York Times* article (February 14, 1984), corroborates the good-student findings after examining the academic records of young Einstein held by Swiss archives. The records confirm that "Einstein was a child prodigy, conversant in college physics before he was 11 years old, a 'brilliant' violin player who got high marks in Latin and Greek." It appears the dull-student notion is much ado about "relativity"!

ELASTICITY

"Springiness" is not just a property of springs, as many are inclined to believe. When physicist Robert Hooke, in 1678, published what he called "The True Theory of Elasticity," he noted that even solid materials are springy to some extent— they stretch under tension and shrink under compression. Thus not only the long cables of a bridge stretch and compress but also the concrete pillars that support the steel cables. The downward compressing of the concrete pillars is a mere fraction of an inch, but on a five-mile-long bridge, cables can stretch as much as five feet. A tall skyscraper such as Chicago's Sears Tower bends several inches off the vertical, and considerably more in high winds. The elasticity of solid rock plays a significant role in earthquakes. If doubt still lingers, consider the 1912 creation by scientists J. D. Birchall and Anthony Kelly, who made an actual spring out of cement.

ELEPHANTS

Bad movies and books written by overly imaginative authors (Frank Buck's African lore) have all contributed to a plethora of misinformation about the big lovable beast—the elephant. Because of their large size, the notion exists that elephants often live to ages of up to 80 to 100. Half of that age comes closer to the truth, the average age being between 38 and 48 years old. The oldest recorded elephant life span was 69, attained by a female Indian elephant living in Australia. Another myth is that the mouse is the master of the elephant. Pure squeeko! The only basis for this belief is that on occasion mice have been known to run up the trunk of the big animals, causing them to panic and act erratically in an attempt to extricate the raunchy rodent. Nor are those avid elephanters who keep track of Africa's wild herds very impressed with the stories about elephant graveyards. They've seen too many bones and carcasses strewn all over Africa to believe that elephants have the slightest propensity for choosing their own burial sites. Besides, elephants have a habit (not yet fully understood) of bone scattering, which means if they really cared a big bunch about burial sites they probably would leave their loved ones intact. Moreover, elephants are known to eat bones for their calcium content. Finally, in defense of those who would attribute strange habits to elephants, it has been well documented that elephants do actually remove tusks from their dead comrades and carry them to outlying areas—perhaps as inherited contempt for poachers!

ELEPHANT TUSKS

Although it is generally believed that ivory elephant tusks are separate protrusions from the elephant's skull, they are actually extensions of the upper second-incisor teeth—probably the most extreme example of buckteeth found anywhere. Another misconception is that the only source of ivory is from elephant tusks. Actually, the teeth of the hippopotamus, walrus, narwhal, sperm whale, and some types of wild boars and warthogs are all recognized as ivory.

EVENING STAR

There are at least a couple of things wrong with the term "evening star." The first flaw is that it really isn't a star, rather it is Venus, the early-night planet that preens prettily over the western horizon not by its own light, but from the grace of the sun. Being the closest planet to our sun, it is thus within our own solar system. (True stars, other than our own sun, are not part of our solar system.) Venus often gets mistaken for that other so-called evening star—Mercury. When they lie *west* of the sun and can be seen before sunrise, they are called morning stars. But whether morning or evening, they are still planets.

EVERGLADES

To most non-Floridians the vast, miasmic swamp in southern Florida known as the Everglades is a sloshy, inhospitable wilderness—an incredibly forbidding bog infested with alligators, snakes, spindly legged birds, and a tribe or two of unsociable Indians. The Everglades may be all of that, and more, but the region is not really a swamp, it is an imperceptibly *slow-moving river.* The ancient river begins at freshwater Lake Okeechobee, pours over 3,500 square miles of salt grass, rotting leaves, seed covers, and roots, meanders southwest through a massive mangrove forest, and finally picks up speed down a shallow escarpment leading to the Gulf of

Mexico. Its width of up to seventy miles makes the Everglades the widest swamp (oops!) river in the world.

EXERCISE WARM-UP

Why do some joggers start their workouts by pushing over trees? Or it seems that's what they're attempting to do. Joggers say they're *stretching their muscles!* Well, hold on now! According to current information from the sports-medicine experts, stretching cold muscles (especially on a cold day) can lead to *injuries,* not benefits. The best way to prepare for jogging, bicycling, tennis, or any other exercise, say these fitness gurus, is to warm up the muscles *first,* then try pushing over that oak tree.

EXCISION

Most everyone is aware of the practice of circumcision, where the whole or part of the foreskin of the penis is cut away. (Ouch!) But few know of its gender counterpart—excision, or female circumcision, where there is a cutting away of the whole or part of the external genitalia. And, surprisingly, it is not a rare practice but is done in a number of places, except perhaps North America. Especially is it practiced by people in cultures considered to be backward civilizations—New Guinea, parts of Australia, Africa, the Malay archipelago, Ethiopia, etc. Islamic people of Asia and India are also known to practice excision. Some anthropologists have concluded that female circumcision actually antedates male circumcision.

EYE COORDINATION

Because we never see a person willfully move one eyeball independently of the other, we tend to think it is impossible. However, with practice, it can be done, and there are numerous grobian contortionists who are more than willing to perform the purposeless feat for you. Parallel focusing (independent eye wandering) in *newborns* happens most of the time. However, within about six weeks "binocular vision" begins to develop and within several months normal eye coordination is established. But with practice, for whatever silly reason you may want to be cross-eye proficient, you can become a baby again and cross your eyes.

F

FAIRS

Today's state and county fairs, with their numerous forms of exhibits and entertainment, are primarily *secular* in nature, but they weren't originally conceived to be secular. In fact, in ancient times, all fairs were productions connected with *religious* matters. In the time of the Phoenicians (beginning about 1000 B.C.), the Arabic city of Mecca was the scene of great festivals held by the pilgrims who journeyed to Mecca for religious reasons. But fairs actually have much earlier beginnings—dating back to ancient tribal periods. Tribes who were often at war with each other would gather at designated spots to exchange goods at the "fair ground" where they would declare a momentary truce, as they regarded such places as being holy ground. America's fairs date back to about the early 1800s, but some fairs in England—the Bartholomew Fair of London and the Sturbridge Fair near Cambridge, for instance—had runs of over 700 years, dating back to the year 1133. The Sturbridge Fair continued up to 1934.

FAMILY NAMES

It is thought by many that multiple names given to people was a Western permutation; however, the earliest use of multiple names dates back not to the Western world, but to ancient China. The Emperor Fushi is said to have decreed the use of family names, or surnames, about the year 2852 B.C. Perhaps if they had telephone directories in that day one could expect to see a listing of 10 million Fong Ling Longs. At any rate, the custom of the so-called surname didn't come into *common* use until the late Middle Ages.

FAT AND THIN

This entry may not appeal to the lite and lean people but perhaps it should. The notion that being fat is unhealthy has been acceptable medical dogma for many years, but research by prestigious health and mortality-study groups, including the well-regarded Framingham studies, shows that being *thin* leads to *earlier* death than does being heavy. The finding that skinnies have higher mortality rates than their portly counterparts came from a continued analysis of 5,209 men and women of Framingham, Massachusetts, who participated in a heart-disease study from 1948 to 1972, a period sufficiently long for veracity. The study showed that danger lurked quite equally for both thin women and heavy women, but among men the lightest group had the highest death rate and the heaviest group had the lowest. The standard actuarial tables reported by insurance companies in earlier years indicated that the higher a person's weight the greater the risk of death. But in 1980 a reexamination of the more recent portion of that data supported the finding of increased mortality at weights more than 20 percent below average. Reubin Andres of the National Institute on Aging throws in an international kicker: Andres reviewed sixteen studies on the relationship between obesity and mortality in groups throughout the world and found that none of the studies linked obesity to early death. Moreover, he found data in many of the studies which indicated that the girthy people in a given population actually had the longest survival times. This shouldn't give the heavyweights any reason to try to achieve their critical mass, however, because they are still candidates for a variety of risks and complications, including diabetes, high blood pressure, cardiovascular and gall bladder problems, and degenerative diseases, plus the increased chances of something going afoul during surgery.

FAX (FACSIMILE) MACHINES

Those incredible fax copiers that send letters, graphics, pictures, and café lunch orders over telephone lines have moved into the consumer sector like a silent tidal wave starting in the mid 1980s. For most people, the fax idea is a brand new, first-ever development. But that assumption is false! The first crude fax machine was patented much too early for anyone living today to have seen it. The patent was granted back in 1843 to a Scottish clock maker, Alexander Bain. (Fax equipment in use over a century and a half ago? Come on, now!) Bain's equipment could transmit written information over wires using grounded metal letters at the sending end, scan the information by use of an electrical head, translate it into electrical signals, and record it on electrochemical paper at the receiving end. All that in he middle of the last century! In 1902, further facsimile developments were introduced by a German physicist, Arthur Korn, who invented the method of photoelectric scanning. Well, why in the blazes did it take so long for this old fax creature to heat up in the new world? Ever heard of the 1968 *Carterfone* decision? In essence, it was a decision made by the FCC to require telephone companies—the fax owners—to allow access to their public-switched telephone network by nontelephone equipment products such as facsimile machines. Prior to this decision, facsimile machines were under tariff from the telephone companies and one couldn't actually own his own equipment. But while the rest of the world piddled along, the Japanese were working behind their rice-paper vanity screens with incredible schemes to capture the fax machine market all by themselves, which is precisely what they did. Since 1984, more than 90 percent of all fax machines have come from Japan.

FEDERAL GOVERNMENT BUREAUCRACY
We often hear about the ever-ballooning federal government workforce, the bulk of which is comprised of the civil-service establishment—a colossal federal growth industry plugging numberless people into newly created jobs. But actually, the trend has been in the *opposite* direction. The federal bureaucracy in 1949 consisted of 2.1 million workers. By 1980, while the country had grown by 70 million people, the federal force was augmented by a modest 750,000 people. From 1940 to 1985 the *percentage* of workers in the federal workforce actually decreased. In short, the population numbers have actually outpaced the growth of the establishment. It is the *state* governments that have grown turgid with an influx of new workers (212 percent since 1950, as opposed to only 27 percent for the federal government).

FEDERAL RESERVE BANKING SYSTEM
Despite its suggestive title, the Federal Reserve System—the central banking system in the United States—is not an arm of the government. It was initially established as an independent agency that was not to be controlled by the executive branch of the government nor by Congress. Rather it is a privately owned banking consortium whose notes are not backed by gold but by the assets and productivity of the American people. Initially the Fed had to make an annual how-goes-it report to Congress, but usually only as a formality. Each of the twelve Federal Reserve Banks is a private business with its own president and board of directors. The Board of Governors of the Fed, including its chairperson, are, however, appointed by the President of the United States

with the approval of Congress. As to significant money matters affecting the country, the President can twist the chairperson's arms, but the chairperson needn't cry "uncle!"

FILMMAKING

When one thinks of the film industry, certainly the name Hollywood comes to mind. The glamour capital has indeed made a prodigious number of motion pictures, and still does, but the United States is no longer King Kong of the film industry. Nor is any other leading industrialized nation. The country that leads all others in full-length film production is, much to everybody's surprise—India! In 1981, India produced a total of 737 full-length movies, well over twice that of runner-up Japan and over three times the U.S. output. The United Kingdom, the traditional redoubt of drama, made a mere 41 full-length movies during 1981, about the same as Poland. Ghana made one movie, but don't look for it at the Cannes Film Festival.

FINGERNAILS

The white spots observed on the fingernails of many people are often, but erroneously, thought to be caused by a calcium deficiency. Your grandmother may have given you that bit of misinformation, bless her concerned little heart, but actually, those spots are nothing more than bruises from hits and knocks received in the course of your daily activities. Another little-known fact is that nail growth doesn't take place at the end of the fingernails and toenails, but at the base of the nail—under the skin. The exposed nails (mainly hardened dead skin cells) are forced from that *live* area along the top of the digits, extending out as long as one cares to let them grow. (Caution: they start curling after a few months, so don't expect to get a typing job.) A third misconception about fingernails is that they continue to grow after death. Body-snatchers know that just isn't so; they only appear to have lengthened because the cuticle around them shrinks.

FISH NEVER DROWN
When fish are in their natural element, why should they drown? The answer is quite simple. Fish, which need oxygen as well as land animals, can indeed drown if sufficient oxygen is denied them. Gills—the respiratory organs of fish, crustaceans, mollusks, worms, and some insects—do the same work as the lungs do for assimilating oxygen (only from a different medium). That's why aquarium fish will eventually go belly-up even in fresh water if sufficient oxygen isn't provided, and is the reason aerators are placed in fish tanks.

FLAMMABLE/INFLAMMABLE
If the word *flammable* means "that which will burn," then surely the antithesis of *flammable* must be *inflammable*. However, such is not the case. In past years petroleum trucks were usually inscribed with the warning sign INFLAMMABLE, which did nothing but beg the question: "Will the petroleum inside the tank burn or won't it?" A check of your dictionary will tell you that both words—*flammable* and *inflammable*—mean the same thing, to wit: "that which is easily set on fire, will burn readily or quickly, is combustible." Although both words have the same meaning, trucks now usually bear the inscription FLAMMABLE.

FLYING FISH
The so-called flying fish of ocean waters do not actually fly at all, as do birds. Rather they boom out of the water at an accelerated speed that allows them to *glide* through the air, using their motionless fins only as wings and stabilizers. This also pertains to squirrels, frogs, lemurs, and several other supple-membrane animals that seem to want the best of both worlds—ground and air.

FOOD AND DRUG ADMINISTRATION RECALLS AND SEIZURES

Occasionally we read about "FDA recalls" and "FDA seizures." Just what do these terms mean? Government intervention and enforcement, probably? Probably not! Contrary to public opinion, the FDA is not empowered to force manufacturers to *recall* defective or dangerous products from any of their inventories. If the threat of bad publicity isn't sufficient to cause the profit-motivated manufacturer to voluntarily withdraw questionable items from its shelves, they can remain there until court action forces such an action. (Or until hell freezes over, whichever comes sooner.) FDA seizures, on the other hand, can be made on any *adulterated* or *mislabeled* food, drug, device, or cosmetic product.

FOOD LABELING

The 1990 Food Labeling Law was enacted by Congress to make it easier for buyers to analyze exactly what food processors put into food, thus allowing for a higher level of nutritional savvy on the part of the consumer. However, many misconceptions and labeling gimmicks still remain to confuse us, including the following:

a. "Cholesterol-free" or "no cholesterol." While products labeled this way cannot have any cholesterol, such labels can lead people to assume that the product *once* had cholesterol. Many foods such as peanut butter and margarine are advertised as being cholesterol-free. Big deal! They never had any to start with. Only *animal* products contain cholesterol.

b. "New." Foods with labels reading "new" give consumers the impression that they have recently been added to the market inventory, but foods, other than meat and poultry, can be "new" as long as the product exists, if the manufacturer so desires.

c. "Lite." Today's food-processing companies have picked up on the consumer signals quite well and are responding by

producing numerous so-called lite and luscious offerings,
ostensibly lower in calories, fats, and other undesirable
ingredients. But does the term *lite* really mean anything?
The word *lite* can refer to calories, taste, color, texture, less
breading, or anything else, making it questionable as to just
what is being done for that bulging torso or hardened string
of arteries. Incidentally, the same applies to lite beer or wine;
here the word can also refer to taste, color, or body.

d. "Low-fat." Does your carton of 2 percent milk really
contain only 2 percent fat, or is that just another fatuous
misrepresentation in the bogus business of labeling? The
answer is both yes and no! It is indeed only 2 percent fat by
weight, but a whopping 35 percent fat by *calories.* Fat is very
light and fluffy but dense in calories (nine calories per gram
compared to four in proteins or carbohydrates). When
cream rises to the top of whole milk, it equates to only 4
percent of the milk's volume by weight, the other 96 percent
being below the cream line. But that 4 percent cream equals
53 percent of the total calories in the milk. To make this
clearer, remember that milk is 89 percent water; therefore,
the cow-milk people are actually crediting water as having fat
when it doesn't. Check out the chart below:

Whole milk = 3.3% fat by weight / 53% fat by calories
2% milk =   2.0% fat by weight / 35% fat by calories
1% milk =   1.0% fat by weight / 22% fat by calories
Skim milk = −1.0% fat by weight / 4.0% fat by
             calories

The same thing applies to the so-called low-fat lunch meats
and sliced cheese. Lunch meats may claim to be 96 percent
fat-free, but 30 percent of the meat's total calories are fat
calories. The four fat grams in a piece of lite cheese (with
seventy calories) amounts to a staggering 51 percent fat
content by calories.

e. "Natural" and "all-natural." Probably the most overused, misunderstood, and deceptive labeling gimmick found in the food industry is the use of the word *natural*. What kind of a flimflam word is *natural*? Snake venom is natural! Cholesterol is natural! Saturated fat is natural! That doesn't mean they're good for you. But since the word has no legal meaning, and since good health is somehow defined by these kinds of legitimized words, food processors can fill up their cornucopias with a lot of nothing-but-natural malarkey about practically anything they produce, although the term means very little. Actually many foods labeled "natural" may be highly processed and contain large amounts of fat, preservatives, and even artificial flavorings. They aren't necessarily good for you, but they're natural. Only in the case of meat and poultry does the word *natural* have any kind of meaningful definition, all relating to artificial coloring, flavoring, preservatives, or synthetic ingredients, which are FDA no-no's! All of which means you may be better off regarding the word *natural* as a *caveat* rather than a reassurance.

f. Non-dairy creamers. You are eating that luscious cream-topped pumpkin pie and you think you're home safe as far as calories are concerned. But here's a verboten for you: Non-dairy creamers contain one of the most highly saturated fats that can be added to food—coconut oil. It's even more saturated than milk fat, and though non-dairy creamers contain no cholesterol, they're loaded with as many calories as light cream. So you may want to skip that second serving of dessert. But shucks, when it's Thanksgiving Day, live it up!

g. "Salt-free" or "no salt added." These terms are supposed to mean that no table salt (sodium chloride) has been added *during processing*, but the product could have significant amounts of naturally occurring sodium or high levels from substances added for preservation, leavening, or other purposes—monosodium glutamate, sodium bicarbonate, or sodium saccharin. Moreover, any food containing less than five milligrams of salt can legally be labeled as being sodium-free.

h. Whole wheat bread. You've got to especially watch those flaky bread labels marked WHEAT BREAD, or even some of the loaves marked WHOLE WHEAT BREAD. In bread (our classic food staple) we also have a classic misconception (not to mention a misrepresentation). First of all, *wheat* bread, which may look somewhat like whole wheat bread because of its brownish color, is little more than white bread in basic composition—a mix of about 75 percent white and 25 percent whole wheat flour. Bakeries have clever ways of milling and massaging their bread to fool the eye and palate. Even some breads labeled *whole* wheat are often not fully whole wheat in content. The bread label may indicate wheat flour, but unless the words "whole wheat" are shown *first* on the list of ingredients, you may be getting neither whole wheat nor the whole truth; just baker's rhubarb!

FOSTER, Stephen

Few would argue that Stephen Collins Foster was one of America's best-loved Southland songwriters. Certainly he had to be a southerner who loved his black-eyed peas, yellow corn, and mellow grits. Otherwise how could he have written all those southern sounds that came right out of the plantation fields? Well, he wrote them because he was an unusually gifted balladeer, not because of any southern exposure he may have had. Actually, Foster was a northerner from Lawrenceville, Pennsylvania, and only ventured to Dixieland for a short while in 1852. He even lived in New York City the last four years of his life and died there, reportedly due to poverty and alcoholism. Also, contrary to the tradition of most light-music composers who didn't write the lyrics for their songs, Foster was his own lyricist for most of the two hundred songs he published during his lifetime. He is indeed one of our national treasures.

FRANKENSTEIN

The frightful figure we've come to know as Frankenstein wasn't the name given him by Mary Shelley, his literary creator. Victor Frankenstein was the *student* who created, out of materials stolen from a dissecting laboratory, an unnamed monster that eventually turned on him. Books and movies have given Frankenstein his classic name.

FRANKLIN, Benjamin, and His Kite

To suggest that Benjamin Franklin's kite, flown in a thunderstorm in 1752, wasn't hit by lightning (resulting in his identifying lightning as electricity) would be regarded as heretical—punishable by a thunderbolt from on high. But, in fact, the kite was *not* struck by lightning as is generally thought. What actually took place during that famous experiment was something far short of lightning. There is always a flow of electrons between the atmosphere and the ground that is amplified during a storm, and Franklin's kite string provided a channel for that energy flow, as evidenced by the spark that jumped from the key to his finger. These phenomena are not to be confused with the megasurge of electricity that builds up to become a full-blown lightning strike. Had the lightning bolt picked Benjamin's kite as its target, it would have quickly fried poor Franklin and the world would have been deprived of all the remarkable things he accomplished later on in his life. Strangely, his own personal written account of the kite experiment wasn't forthcoming until 1788, although it was earlier recorded by Joseph Priestley in his *History and Present State of Electricity,* published fifteen years after Franklin's kite flight.

FREEDOM OF INFORMATION ACT

It would be nice to know *everything* that's in the federal government's files, but only a dreamer would expect the 1976 Freedom of Information Act to give him unlimited access to *all* information under the government's stewardship, as some have been led to believe. The act—which applies to federal information collected on sundry subjects, from civil rights compliance to government product testing, and which allows access to information regardless of why it is needed and how it will be used—is *conditional*. All the government need do to *deny* giving up information from its prodigious database is to explain why such information *cannot* be provided. In fact, the fed even has a clearing house to sort out what it wants to divulge and what it doesn't.

FREUD, Sigmund

Although Sigmund Freud's brief studies and internship at the University of Vienna gave him limited experience at that school's psychiatric clinic, the Austrian-born physician and founder of psychoanalysis was not a practicing psychiatrist or psychologist as is commonly thought, but a *neurologist*. (Some critics believe he had more talent for metaphor than for medicine.) Although his life's work was directed toward unraveling the twisted ropes of the mentally unstable, his own psyche had a few knots of its own. During his mid-forties, realizing he was growing older, Freud was thrown by his troubled "id" into a period of deep depression wherein he even refused to be photographed. And although Freud's touchstone theories have served as a basis for clinical practice during much of the past century, his old "black-couch" method of analysis would be regarded today as *Mad*-magazine material by most clinicians.

FRONT-WHEEL DRIVE VERSUS REAR-WHEEL DRIVE

Claims about front-wheel-drive automobiles performing better in snow and ice than rear-wheel-drive cars may be accurate in regard to certain aspects of vehicle handling, but the truth is that once traction is broken, front-wheel drive is no more effective in snow and ice than rear-wheel drive.

FUNNY BONE
There's really nothing intrinsically funny about a "funny bone" other than the humor elicited when someone else sustains that sharp pain in the vicinity of his elbow. Nor does the pain have anything to do with the bone itself. It actually results from striking a nerve that runs close to the tip of the elbow. A considerable amount of pain can be felt just by pressing down on that crazy nerve. But maybe the name of that bone in the upper arm does offer some basis for humor; after all, it's called the humerus.

G

GALILEO AND THE LEANING TOWER OF PISA
Legend has it that Galileo dropped a bullet and a cannonball from the Leaning Tower of Pisa to prove that all bodies fall with the same acceleration. But that legend skates on thin ice. Galileo's conclusions regarding falling bodies were clearly stated as a result of his careful experiments on the speed of balls rolling down *inclined planes.*

GANDHI, Mahatma
Although the first given name of India's patron saint of passive resistance is generally thought of as being "Mahatma," such was not his actual name. Rather it was "Mohandas," a name bestowed upon him by his venerating followers, the meaning of which is "Great Soul." Another

general misconception about the tunic-clad stoic is that he always denied himself the sweet fruits of indulgence. The fact is, as a teenager, he had his bouts with rebellion—eating meat with Muslim friends, smoking cigarettes, and stealing—sins that he confessed to his dying father, which gave him a feeling of absolution resulting in his resolve to consecrate his life to the welfare of his fellow man.

GAS, Weight of

If a small amount of colored gas were emitted into an average-size room, you would notice that it spreads upward and outward in apparent defiance of gravity, leaving you with the belief that the gas, along with the air in the room, has no perceptible weight. (Surely there's no weight involved with rising gas?) Surprisingly, the gas in that room weighs approximately 100 pounds.

GENERIC DRUGS

We often hear that taking generic drugs is sometimes risky, and a lot of people have queasy feelings about using them. So let's find out just what a generic drug is: A pharmaceutical company develops a drug on which it obtains a patent for seventeen years, giving it exclusive rights on all sales of that product. (This can be extended for up to five years in some cases.) But after that the competition can mix up a barn-full of its own, put its brand on it, and enter the hard-sell rat race, hoping its copy proves to be as popular as the original. Is the drug just as potent, just as effective, and just as safe as the original? Maybe knowing who provides the quality control would raise our confidence! This much should be understood: All drug manufacturers, whether they produce brand-name or generic products, must comply with the same FDA-mandated standards. So the only difference between the two is found in the price—from 30 to 80 percent lower for the generics. So despite some rare problems with generics (about as frequent as with the brand-name products), you may feel at ease knowing that more than 8,000 generics are currently sold with FDA approval to millions of people every day; that all Veterans Administration hospitals use them, and that when the President of the United States gets medications at Walter Reed Hospital, he may get generics just as others do. Essentially, "generic" simply means the drug is no longer protected by trademarks. And if you trust the FDA on the originals you should be able to trust it with the generics. The copy must be shown to be the bio-equivalent of the original drug as to substance, blood absorption rate, etc. The spooky part in the eyes of the pill-taker is the confidence factor.

GENETIC/CONGENITAL

There tends to be a lot of confusion regarding the words *genetic* and *congenital*, both of which stem from the Greek word meaning "birth." But although these terms share the same base, they mean strikingly different things. A genetic defect is a condition that is determined at the moment of conception, when each parent gives the new entity half its genetic makeup. Genetic conditions have the potential for being passed from one generation to the next. On the other hand, the word *congenital* describes conditions that develop after conception, i.e., throughout the gestation period, but which are not inheritable. Many congenital conditions result from such things as poor prenatal nutrition, alcohol use, smoking, etc.

GENGHIS KHAN

Even though most of what we hear of the man paints him as a ruthless and exploitative madman, actually Genghis, whose real name was Temujin, meaning "Ironsmith," was not without redeeming virtues. Despite all his mischief, he was essentially a spiritual person, a man driven by the conviction that he was commanded by the "Eternal Blue Sky"—the highest supernatural power the old Mongolian religion recognized—to carry out his fateful missions. As to his death, it

appears we have another misconception: It is generally
believed Genghis Khan was killed in some sort of military
action, but he actually suffered a rather ignominious demise—the old sod fell off his horse.

GERMS

Despite our traditional understanding of the germs which we
have come to identify as minute biological buggers that
invade and infect our bodies, the word *germ* is not really a
medical term at all. It simply means something that is
capable of growing into something larger—the germ of the
wheat kernel, for instance. Because such a term has
seemingly endless references, science prefers to classify
germs as bacteria, protozoa, bacilli, or other types of
microbes.

GERONIMO

Was this legendary Apache warrior a cold-blooded killer, or,
as perceived by General George Crook, "one of the greatest
Americans who ever lived"? There's a lot we don't know
about Geronimo, first of which is that his Indian name was
Goyathlay. The Mexicans named him Geronimo, meaning
Jerome. (Know any fierce Jeromes?) Ask most people what
happened to Geronimo and they usually surmise that he was
killed by government soldiers. But Geronimo wasn't killed by
anyone. After the feds chased his fanny all over the southwest and into Mexico, they finally nabbed him, and he was
sent to Fort Sill, where he modified his behavior (if you can't
lick 'em, join 'em!) and became a Christian (he joined the
Dutch Reformed Church but was later expelled because of
his penchant for gambling). He also worked for the U.S.
government at the fort, until he died at the age of eighty.
Ironically, it wasn't government soldiers who finally captured
the marauding maverick but Apache Indian scouts serving in
the U.S. Army under General Nelson A. Miles.

GLACIERS ON THE EQUATOR?
Most people perceive glaciers to be slow-moving rivers of ice found only in the North and South Polar regions—in Greenland, Norway, Iceland, the European Alps, and the mountains of the western United States. But glaciers can be anomalies. Mount Kenya, for instance, an extinct volcanic cone in Kenya in East Africa, has vast permanent glaciers of its own reaching high up its 17,040-foot peak and is, as most people are aware, close to the equator.

GLASS
Although glass can be formed into definite shapes and is brittle enough to shatter, it nevertheless is not a solid but a liquid. The length of time it takes to measure the flow of glass depends primarily on its shape. A long thin glass rod supported at its ends will sag in a few weeks' time, while thicker glass may take hundreds or even thousands of years to show significant change. But change will inevitably come. Another hazy peculiarity about glass relates to its beginnings. Science books tell us that the making and use of glass dates back to the earliest periods of civilization. But it actually goes back much further than that—to the time of the formation of the earth by the forces of nature. The prime ingredient for making glass is sand. We have evidence that natural glass was made from sand by lightning long before there were people on earth. The lightning's intense heat melted the sand, which cooled into glass tubes with forks and branches the shape of the lightning strike itself, leaving entire forests of what has come to be called "frozen lightning." This hasn't got a thing to do with what this paragraph started out to prove, but I thought you might want to add "frozen lightning" to your stock of knowledge. You can never tell when you'll need such information!

GLASS CUTTERS
The term "glass cutter" is somewhat of a misnomer. No glass cutter actually "cuts" glass, rather it *fractures* it. A glass cutter is a device with a handle and an axle on one end that holds a small steel wheel which makes a nearly-imperceptible groove in the glass as it turns. (It also makes a dumb noise that defies description.) Anyway, when the right amount of pressure is applied in the right place, the fracture begins to "run" and the glass separates—ideally on the scored line. (Inexperienced glass fracturers who don't know the score often score their fingers.)

GLOWWORM
The little wingless glowworm with the flickering green-yellow light on its caboose is not really a worm but an insect. Such fireflies are often referred to as lightning bugs or lightning beetles. While we're on the subject of worms, it should be noted also that the silkworm is not a worm but a caterpillar—the larva of a moth.

GOGH, Vincent van
He was only able to sell a single painting during his lifetime. Today you would need a money magnet to afford one of his paintings. Poor old van Gogh, so deranged that he cut off one of his ears and mailed it to a passionate prostitute! (Actually, it was only the lobe of the ear.) Was van Gogh really a kook, as most people have come to believe? Probably not. Van Gogh was indeed eccentric, but history has apparently painted the Dutchman into a distorted Rorschach corner. Recent research reveals that the artist for the most part was a rational and productive man, clearly in control of his reasoning ability, as attested by 796 letters written by him to his family and friends between 1884 and his suicide in 1890, at age thirty-seven. The truth is, the wretched soul was physically ailing during much of his productive life—handicapped by a disabling inner-ear disorder called Ménière's

disease which left him with severe tinnitus (ringing ears), chronic vertigo, and depression. At any rate, biography today takes a more studied and forgiving view of the man's irrational behavior as being perhaps his own way of mitigating the pain. Another fact about van Gogh's personal life that tends to support the new evidence is that his first legitimate vocation was that of a preacher, evangelist, and peripatetic missionary who labored among the impoverished coal miners in the region of southwest Belgium.

GOLD

Contrary to public opinion, Fort Knox has not been the place of the most activity in gold in the United States. Most daily gold transactions are handled at the U.S. Assay Office in New York, which keeps a working stock of around a thousand tons. Fort Knox is broached only when the Assay Office is overflowing (as was the case in the 1930s and 1940s) or when it is running short (as it was during the 1950s and 1960s). And in spite of all the fables about gold being used by the ancients, this highly prized metal hasn't been available in any real quantity until the past 130 years. Only about ten thousand tons of gold had been mined from the beginning of time up to the mid-nineteenth century. Another interesting thing about gold is that in ancient times, spices were the treasure king of the world, not gold or gem jewelry or diamonds.

GOLD JEWELRY MANUFACTURING

With all the jewelry coming out of the Orient these days one would think most *gold* jewelry comes from one of the countries of that area, but it is the Italians who lead the field in gold jewelry manufacturing. The communities of Arezzo, Vicenza, Bassano del Grappa, and Valenza make close to a quarter of the world's gold jewelry. They lead the world in *amore,* why not gold?

GOOSE-STEP MARCHING
Although it is a common belief that the moronic, peg-legged goose-step style of marching originated with the Nazis during Hitler's Germany, it was by no means original with them. The goose-step march (or strut, or whatever that witless ambulation is supposed to be) has been around for millennia—used by armies many years prior to World War II. It is still used today in some Middle Eastern countries and was used by Soviet soldiers pacing back and forth in front of the former U.S.S.R.'s National Memorial Cemetery.

G.O.P.
As much as Republicans would prefer the initials "G.O.P." to mean *Government of the People,* the acronym simply means "Grand Old Party."

GORBACHEV, Mikhail
Mikhail Gorbachev is familiar to most everyone these days but, contrary to what they generally suppose, "Gorbachev" is not his *social last name.* In the Russian culture, the social last name is the middle name. Thus the customary way to address Mikhail Sergeyevich Gorbachev (vulgarized as "Gorby") would be "Mikhail Sergeyevich." Similarly, when we refer to the late Chinese communist leader "Chairman Mao," we're not calling Mao Tse-tung by his first name. That's because in China, the second name *is* the first name. But alas, poor Mao is dead, and we'll never get the opportunity to address him properly.

GORILLAS BEATING THEIR CHESTS
When it comes to gorillas beating their chests, perhaps the hand actually *is* quicker than the eye. The staccato thumping happens so fast we don't really pay attention to how old King Kong pulls it off. The illusion is that he is using his clenched fists, but the rapid popping noise is actually made by the big fellow using his open, slightly-cupped hands, not his fists.

And why does the jungle faker bang on his chest in the first place? It's all either sexual or territorial. Something else is usually misunderstood about the gorilla: it isn't always the macho male who does the thumping; the ladies do it too, though less frequently and with more gentility.

GREENLAND

For anyone desiring to visit Greenland, the world's largest island, you may be interested to know that virtually none of the island's terrain is green. The only greening to be seen is in the coastal areas, but for only a short duration during the summer.

GUINEA PIGS

The cute but unfortunate guinea pig (Cavia porcellus) has at least three strikes against it: First, the little cavies aren't pigs, they are rodents. Second, they don't come from Guinea, they come from South America; and third, they aren't the animals mostly used for experimental purposes. Mice, rats, rabbits, and chickens all out—guinea pig the guinea pig.

HALO

The luminous ring or disk of light surrounding the heads or bodies of sacred figures such as saints depicted in religious paintings was originally not a Christian symbol but a pagan one. According to etymologists, even the word itself doesn't trace back to any object of Christian significance.

HARLEQUIN
Pity the poor harlequin. Or should we? For sure, most people have an erroneous concept of the Middle Ages court jester. In the early years of sixteenth-century Italian comedy this hapless buffoon didn't get the respect now accorded Rodney Dangerfield. Once regarded as a wily and covetous comic servant—cowardly, superstitious, and plagued by a continual lack of money and food—his cleverness wore down his critics, and by the early seventeenth century, the harlequin clowned himself into the good graces of respectable society, becoming a faithful and patient valet, gracious and even amorous.

HAWAII
In spite of its many superlatives, Hawaii is not without its misconceptions. Several are listed below:

a. Aloha. While in Hawaii you would do well to do as the Hawaiians do—adopt the word *aloha*. But understand that it means more than "hello," "greetings," "welcome," and "farewell," which most people know of. Rather it's a word that has over a *hundred* definitions, and is used not only in Hawaii but in all of the Polynesian countries.

b. Cattle ranches. Home on the range in Hawaii? Much to the surprise of many people, Hawaii has the largest *single-owner* cattle ranch in the United States. Cattle were first introduced into Hawaii as early as 1793, out of which evolved the famous Parker Ranch, second in size only to the *corporate* King Ranch of Texas. Approximately 50,000 cattle graze on 225,000 paradisaical acres beneath the mist-shrouded, 13,796-foot-high dormant volcano Mauna Kea and the Kohala Mountains, sprawling west to the windswept Kohala coast. This is no small pig farm, folks; more Hereford cattle are raised on the big island of Hawaii than any other place in the United States.

c. Diamond Head. What about Diamond Head? Does the famous crater mountain overlooking Honolulu really resemble a diamond? Not by a stretch of the imagination! The legendary mountain picked up its name back in the 1800s when British sailors rushed back to their anchored ships with the news that countless diamonds were scattered in plain view all over the place. "Sorry, chaps," declared the ship's captain, "what you saw was only fool's gold, or pyrite."

d. Hawaiian music. Probably no other music is as distinct and ethnically recognizable as Hawaiian music. To most of us, melodies such as "Aloha Oe," "Blue Hawaii," and "Lovely Hula Hands" are as authentic as grass skirts and monkey-faced coconuts. But that lilting, carefree music floating over from the islands isn't part of the art form of pristine Polynesia. Rather it is the result of an acculturation that began in the early nineteenth century with the arrival of Christian missionaries introducing hymn tunes that shaped themselves into what is now a clearly pseudo-Hawaiian music style. Surprisingly, German music is the taproot of most present-day Hawaiian music; however, some of the pure forms of Polynesian music still remain. As for the famous Hawaiian ukulele, it too isn't aboriginal, but is an adaptation of a small guitar called the *bragha,* brought to Hawaii by the Portuguese.

e. Mountains. Opinions to the contrary, the tallest mountain in the world is not Mount Everest, but Mauna Kea, one of five volcanoes on the big island. Measured from its underwater base, Mauna Kea is approximately 33,476 feet tall (according to which reference source one is reading), which makes it about 4,448 feet taller than land-based Everest. Of course, if we wish to split hairs, we'll have to admit that Everest is the tallest *visible* mountain in the world, because more than half of Mauna Kea is *below* the ocean. But mountain measurers say that mountains are measured from their base, whether in water or out of water, so Mauna Kea, whose name means "White Mountain," is still the big one.

f. Native trees. Many of today's poorly researched publications on Hawaii's plant life (in addition to the standard pitch bullhorned by the misinformed tourist guides on the islands) tell us that prior to man's arrival on the islands of Hawaii, the only vegetation to be found were ferns, grasses, and plants, not trees. Not so! Numerous trees of many kinds were standing—the koa haolae, kiawe, kokia, ohia lehua, sandalwood, mamane, and others, including new species that have since been discovered, most of which have become intermixed with trees brought later to the islands by seafaring men from other countries. While it is true that these trees are known to have originally come to Hawaii via ocean and wind currents and by seed-carrying birds (referred to as "long-distance dispersal") they nevertheless antedated man's arrival on the beautiful isles by thousands of years, and therefore are considered indigenous.

g. Poi Far more people *dislike* than *like* the taste of that pasty Hawaiian taro starch called poi, even though it is a highly nourishing food source. People probably wouldn't like poi any more if they found out that the word doesn't refer to a particular food, but is a *description of the manner in which something is produced.* The word *poi* means to twist, squeeze, mash, or pound. Therefore, other vegetables such as sweet potatoes and carrots can also be classified as poi under that definition. The most popular source of poi comes from the taro root. Still don't like it? How about apple poi?

h. Sandwich Islands. Few of the hordes of tourists who visit Hawaii are aware that the original name of the islands was not Hawaii. Initially the islands were referred to as the *Sandwich Islands,* a name conferred upon the small Pacific archipelago in 1778 by Captain James Cook of the British Navy, the unfortunate bloke who first was idolized by the natives only to be murdered by them. Cook named the islands in honor of the Earl of Sandwich, the first Lord of the British admiralty at that time. Many native trees of Hawaii bear a version of the name "Sandwich," as in *Reynoldsia sandwicensis* and sandalwood.

HAY FEVER
The so-called allergic condition referred to as hay fever isn't caused by hay. The principal culprit is ragweed. Actually, there's a lengthy laundry list of things that can raise the misery index for your proboscis and eyes, and they all relate to some kind of natural or human-caused pollution. But hay is exonerated.

HEAD LICE IN CHILDREN
We tend to think that long and dirty hair is a natural haven for head lice, but such is not always the case. The clean-cut kids are just as prone to head lice as the raunchy kids if they are inclined to share each other's combs, headphones, hats, etc. According to the FDA, lice infestations have been on the rise for several years, and are no respecter of age either. Adults can host the lousy lice as well as children, but because adults have generally gotten over those *sharing* habits, their head lice count is down.

HEALTH AND LONGEVITY IN THE UNITED STATES
There is little question that Americans are enjoying a healthier life style than their predecessors of a century ago. But, ironically, our modern-day health improvements do not equate to a significant increase in longevity. The percentage of centenarians living today has not increased virtually at all over former periods.

HEART(S), Human
If a person had two hearts he would most likely be the featured attraction at a freak show. But listen up! Humans *do*

have two hearts! Our main heart, the miracle organ that pumps a railroad tank-car full of blood each day, has a helper—the leg muscles. The leg muscles not only give us mobility, they're also used as servo-mechanisms to assist the main heart to .do all that laborious pumping of blood through the vascular network of our bodies. That's why it's important for joggers, walkers, and swimmers to cool down by continuing at a slower, declining pace. If a person sits down immediately after a strenuous workout, it throws all the pump duty back onto the heart. So, for your health's sake, have a heart and use them both!

HEAT AND TEMPERATURE

Most everyone tends to equate temperature with heat. When it's hot doesn't the thermometer reflect it? Yes, but they're still not the same! Heat and temperature by themselves make sense, but when considered in relation to each other, things begin to get a little murky. That's because the heat content of a given substance depends both upon its mass and its temperature. We say the higher the temperature the more heat an object possesses, but we cannot always say one thing possesses more heat than another thing simply because its temperature is higher. For instance, although a *cupful* of boiling water is by itself hotter than a *pailful* of cool water, the cool water would melt a larger quantity of ice. Consequently the cupful of boiling water contains a smaller amount of heat *despite* its higher temperature.

HINDENBURG

On May 6, 1937, the giant German airship *Hindenburg* burst into a horrifying ball of flames as it prepared to descend at a landing field in Lakehurst, New Jersey. It was the largest airship ever to fly (four times larger than the corporate blimps flying today). The big bag was sumptuously furnished—private staterooms, an elegant dining room, a grand piano, and space for twelve tons of cargo. Although this great tragedy, fortuitously filmed and permanently preserved for posterity, is thought by most people to have killed *all* the passengers aboard, there were, miraculously, many survivors—sixty-two out of ninety-seven passengers who lived to tell their own story. Another mistaken belief concerning the *Hindenburg* (clearly marked with the swastika of Hitler's Nazi Germany) is that it was a blimp; this is not so. The *Hindenburg* was a zeppelin, with a rigid metal framework forming its hull to which separate cells were attached. The cells were filled with flammable hydrogen. Blimps, in contrast, consist of one large gas bag with no framework.

HIPPOCRATES
The Greek physician Hippocrates, widely regarded to be the "father of medicine," may be the most undeserving medical figure of all time. The reason is that nothing certain is known about the fabled physician—his ideas, discoveries, teachings, even the dates of his birth and death. Perhaps he was indeed the genuine article, but the musty manuscripts extant show he was medicine's architect only because the ancient Greek writers *inferred* he was. Also, there is no conclusive evidence to prove that he was the originator of the well-known Hippocratic oath to which graduating medical students swear allegiance.

HITLER, Adolf
Contrary to popular assumption, the maniacal dictator-leader of Nazi Germany, Adolf Hitler, was not German but Austrian. Born in Braunau, Austria, he lived his first thirteen years there before moving to Munich, at which point in his life his political character began to take shape. Another interesting thing generally not known about Der Führer is the fact that he was, for quite a long period of time, only the *junior partner* to Italy's Mussolini in terms of political clout. It wasn't until he cranked up his country's military might that he began to overshadow the beefy Benito.

HOT-AIR BALLOONING

Many people know that France took the lead in developing hot air balloons for occupied flight. Or perhaps people don't! Anyway, ballooners know that Frenchman Jean-François Pilâtre de Rozier was the first person to soar aloft in a hot air balloon on October 15, 1783. (With a name like that, he should be first at something!) They also know that the first occupied *free-floating* balloon flight wasn't made by Pilâtre de Rozier at all, but by a cacophonous entourage of barnyard animals—a rooster, a sheep, and a duck. As for the Frenchman, his balloon wasn't a free floater, but was tethered by an eighty-foot rope. Moreover, the barnyard flight was by far the most heralded and attended. Among the 30,000 viewers watching the flight were King Louis XVI and Queen Marie Antoinette.

HOUSEFLY, Common

This may indeed sound like an airball item for consideration, but if you were to ask the question as to how many legs the common butterfly has, you would find a surprisingly large number of people who would say four. But if you ever get the urge to count fly legs, you would find that the pesty room-raider has *six* legs. But don't feel too bad about your entomological deficiency: The Greek philosopher Aristotle also shortchanged the fly, and his word was taken as fact for over 300 years, until one day someone picked up a fly, examined the winged maggot, and to his amazement found it had six legs. (A good education simply wouldn't be complete without this bit of profundity!)

HUMMINGBIRDS SIPPING NECTAR

Until only recently, it was believed that hummingbirds sucked nectar in much the same manner soda pop is inhaled through a straw. We now know the hustling little hummer actually *licks* the nectar from inside the flower. He does this by use of his long, translucent tongue, which extends out beyond the beak, and gets in about thirteen licks per second, after which he draws back his dulcet delight and swallows. He really gets in his licks toward the end of the feeding season, in preparation for his migration back to warmer climes. And despite the tendency for most birds to fly in protective flocks during their southern journey, this little guy flies solo all the way.

HUNDRED YEARS' WAR

The Hundred Years' War—the senseless war between France and England—was not a continuous, unbroken war, nor did it last for only one hundred years. It started in 1337 and continued to 1453, culminating in the expulsion of the English from France. The above dates, then, tell us the war's duration was 116 years. Furthermore, though the English actually withdrew from France, they retained the port of Calais until 1558. So in terms of the parties completely getting out of each other's hair, the Hundred Years' War stretched out to a Two-Hundred-Twenty-One-Years' War. After that long period of time, people forgot why it started in the first place.

HYENAS

Pity the poor hyena! It isn't likely there will ever be an "adopt-a-hyena" movement anywhere, but the skulking misfit does deserve credits denied by most people. True, it is commonly regarded as a passive carrion lover, seemingly unwilling or afraid to make a kill of anything bigger than itself, but don't sell Mr. Ugly short, especially the spotted hyena—the most macho of the species. According to author Jane Goodall, who was on a first-name basis with all of Africa's wild animals, when in large numbers and when sufficiently hungry (which seems always to be a part of their gluttonous character), hyenas do make aggressive kills of large animals. Equally hungry lions can be harassed into abandoning their kill while the greedy interlopers rip a carcass apart before the hapless lions realize they've been had. Observations have even been made where both lions and hyenas have eaten from the same carcass; however, we should expect the ultimate in terrible table manners at such dining-ins. Dutch scientist Hans Kruuk is even more emphatic in his defense of the unlovable hyena, claiming he is not only a skillful predator but also an intelligent strategist who can instinctively figure out the odds for going on the offensive in pursuit of live game the size of zebras, wildebeests, and water buffalo.

HYPNOSIS

Probably no other subject is so riddled with misconceptions as the science of hypnosis. One of the most prevalent is that the hypnotist takes control of one's mind and programs it like a computer. Not so! Hypnosis is not something the hypnotist *does to you,* but *what you do to yourself* (with the suggestions provided by the hypnotist—the facilitator). In hypnosis, persons don't relinquish their free agency or lose their personal values, nor can they be persuaded to reveal those values to the hypnotist if they choose otherwise. Perhaps the biggest myth about hypnosis is that when persons are under a hypnotic spell they somehow lose consciousness, that they are totally "zonked out," with both eyelids frozen in their sockets. The degree to which a person does appear to be asleep depends only on the level of *focused attention* he has allowed himself to achieve. Most of us enter a quasi-hypnotic state every day in a very natural way. How many times do we find ourselves in never-never land while reading a book, superficially reading the entire page, only to realize we absorbed nary a word because our minds were assessing the day's troubles? Back to the top of the page we go, dreamer! Meanwhile, throughout this seemingly slumberous stupor, life still goes on!

I

ID

Sigmund Freud may have had the rational *ego* instincts to superintend his critical *superego* and his childish *id*, but neither he nor his alter ego actually used those words in his writings. Rather, he preferred expressing the terms in the local dialect.

IDENTICAL TWINS

To say that identical twins are totally and absolutely identical is a bit of a stretch. They do share the same blood type, eye color, and general anatomy, but even these likenesses are not absolute. Identical twins are born from a single egg cell that separates into two parts early in its development, but not until their right- and left-sided characteristics have developed. This makes it possible for the twins to have almost the same characteristics in reverse, which obviously rules out absolute identicalness. Even steel ball-bearings would reveal remarkable dissimilarities if viewed under a powerful microscope.

INDOOR AIR POLLUTION

Home sweet home may not be as sweet as you may suppose. According to a mid-1980s report by the U.S. Consumer Product Safety Commission, the air inside your home is two to four times more polluted than the air outside. The commission identified 150 different chemicals regularly found in homes and linked with cancer, allergies, psychological abnormalities, and birth defects. The subject was again emphasized by the commission in April 1993. So while the public is worried about the ozone, perhaps we should be more concerned about the "homezone."

ILLITERACY/INNUMERACY
An article in a local newspaper described several ninth-grade students in a particular school as being illiterate because of their inability to comprehend simple math problems. Apparently the editor of the newspaper was also illiterate for not knowing the difference between illiteracy and innumeracy. Contrary to what is generally believed, persons lacking math skills (but who are otherwise competent in reading skills) are not illiterate, they are innumerate.

INQUISITION
It would probably be safe to say that most literate persons have some knowledge (albeit vague) of what the so-called "Inquisition" was all about—a practice of the Roman Catholic Church established for tormenting and torching heretics and other malefactors deemed to be "unbelieving" enemies of the Church during the Middle Ages. The practice is most generally referred to as "the" Inquisition, as if it were a *single* historical event, instituting tribunals with dragnet agents dispersed everywhere to shut up apostates and preserve the established order of the holy stewardship. This notion is far from realistic. Inquisitorial activities actually began in the fourth century when Christianity became the officially recognized religion of the Roman Empire under Emperor Constantine, progressing more explicitly with the papal appointment of individual inquisitors pouncing on apostates who failed to eyeball with the Holy See. It wasn't until about the sixteenth century that formal institutions (inquisitions) were set up to demand obedience to orthodox beliefs and maintain ecclesiastical discipline within the Church. Technically there were at least five recognizable inquisitions—medieval, Roman, Spanish, Portuguese, and Venetian, all

with rather distinct inquisitorial objectives. In summary, this whole business of interdicting the infidel spanned hundreds of years, and wasn't finally scrapped until well into the nineteenth century. Also, the Inquisition was not, in the strictest sense, the *action* itself (at first) but the name of the particular tribunal or institution established to carry out the ecclesiastical decree. The acts of the established tribunals gradually came to be regarded as being "the" Inquisition itself.

INTERNAL REVENUE SERVICE

Endless horror stories abound regarding what nefarious means the IRS takes to audit our financial records and grab our money. Some are true, many are not. We've all heard that no income source is out of reach of the shifty tax men, but this is not so. Under federal law, the IRS cannot levy against *all* types of property, the most noteworthy exemptions being unemployment benefits, certain annuity and pension payments, workmen's compensation, deposits to the special treasury fund by military personnel living outside the United States or its possessions, and income that is subject to a prior judgment for court-ordered child support payments. Another misconception about the seemingly sacrosanct publicans and the beleaguered peasantry has to do with assessed penalties. One may face a jail sentence for failing to file a return or committing fraud, but *owing* money to the IRS by itself is not a crime; a tax debtor cannot be sent to the pokey simply for delinquency, regardless of how much is owed. And finally, another myth about the IRS and taxpayer relations is that a taxpayer has no recourse for possible grievances against decisions made by the IRS. The truth is that the IRS is not totally untouchable; it can indeed be taken to court. A person having gone through the Appeals Division with a tax problem who still feels he has a legitimate beef against the IRS can obtain an impartial hearing in the U.S. Tax Court— the separate, independent judicial body established for reviewing tax cases. If he's still not satisfied, the person can appeal to the United States District Court or United States Claims Court. The hitch with these last two courts is that you must *first pay* what the feds say you owe before they'll listen to you. (And don't expect to pick up any interest on the money you've squirreled away while your case is pending!)

IRS AUDITS

Many a taxpayer has been traumatized by the ominous and intimidating IRS notification stating that he is about to receive a tax audit. It is usually standard practice for the notification letter to specify the date at which the taxpayer is to appear. But despite the cardiac-arresting tone of such a notice, it should be understood that the appearance date for audits is appealable, not absolutely firm. Appearing in the Taxpayers Bill of Rights, established by Congress, is the provision that the Internal Revenue Service must select an audit date that is mutually convenient for both the taxpayer and the IRS examiner. A month or longer is not an unreasonable amount of time for the taxpayer to assemble his deductible wits, locate his papers, take care of his personal commitments, and arrange for a professional tax expert to accompany him to the tax audit. Also in the event a taxpayer owes money to the IRS it is not always mandatory that the money be paid immediately. It is possible to *buy* time—forestalling paying the IRS for up to six months by applying for an extension using one of their own forms. (You will probably have to ask for one of these forms; usually they are conveniently out of them.) Finally, one should take with a grain of salt the IRS claim that only a small percentage of taxpayer returns are audited. In truth, *all* returns are computer-audited prior to the lesser number of face-to-face audits finally made. Knowing a few unknowns about taxpayer rights and the fed's policies should bring back the facial color of the most timorous taxpayer who gets nailed with that unspeakable audit.

INVESTMENT IN AMERICA BY FOREIGNERS
Who is really buying up America? Of course, it is Japan! Or is it Korea or Germany? Wrong on all counts! It is the same country that's been the leading investor since colonial days—Great Britain. Furthermore, as of 1989, the friendly chaps from Londontown have actually *extended* their lead over the number-two investor—Japan. The Netherlands also has put its acquisitive hooks into the great American marketplace, so we don't own some of the biggies anymore—hamburger chains, mills, fruit producers, hotel/motels—a real diversity of investment by our overseas trading allies. And there goes another piece of the neighborhood! Perhaps, but there's little need for xenophobia. America still owns more of other countries than they do of ours.

IRON IN AMERICAN DIET
Red meat and green vegetables have always been identified as foods having the highest iron content. But we live in an age of food fortification—cereals, bread, pasta, and baked goods—and whether we like all that added iron or not, the largest source of iron in the American diet is found in grain products.

ISAAC, SON OF ABRAHAM
Paintings of and stories about the legendary Old Testament drama of Abraham offering up his young and innocent son Isaac for human sacrifice usually portray Isaac as being a very young lad at the time he was to be consumed by the fiery fagots on the sacrificial altar. This is because the Book of Genesis refers to him as such. It also makes sense that Isaac must have been quite young in order for his aged father to accomplish the intended sacrifice. But despite the Bible's references to Isaac as being a lad, he had to be a very mature lad indeed—quite possibly in his thirties. Estimates of Isaac's age at that time range anywhere from twenty-five (by the account of Jewish historian Flavius Josephus) to about thirty-

six. Suppose we total the accounts and divide by two; we can ballpark Isaac's age as being at least in the early thirties.

ISRAEL, SON OF JACOB

Father Abraham's grandson Jacob was a righteous man whose name was changed to Israel by the Lord God. And being the prolific man he was, he fathered twelve sons whose progeny later came to be known as the Twelve Tribes of Israel. One of the sons of Israel was named Judah. As the tribe of Judah developed its unique individuality the people eventually came to be identified as Israelites; and here is where we start to fall off the plank! When people think of Israel and the Israelites, they have in mind only Jewish people, or those who have descended from Judah. But it must be remembered, there were eleven other sons, all of whose tribal offspring could rightfully lay claim to being called Israelites (having all come from father Jacob—or Israel). Hence to apply the designation "Israel" and "Israelites" only to the Jews is erroneous, since they constituted only one tribe—the small Kingdom of Judah—when Israel was divided. The followers of Ephraim and Manasseh, sons of Joseph, constituted the large Kingdom of Israel or Ephraim, and were as much the children of Israel as were the Jews.

IVAN THE TERRIBLE

Although poor Ivan will probably never live down his evil name, the infamous first czar of Russia, nicknamed "The Terrible," was no more brutal than most of the rulers during that long Russian czarist period. Actually his nickname is a mistranslation of the Russian word *grozny*, which relates to the phrase "awe-inspiring." In most every aspect, Ivan was an overachiever—a skilled writer, political critic, devout defender of the Orthodox faith, and composer of prayers and church music. Although the facts of his hatchet-man ruthlessness cannot be denied (he even ordered a nobleman's tongue cut out for uttering rude words), objective history reveals that when judged within the context of the ruling justice of his day, Ivan's actions were no more extreme than those of rulers elsewhere.

J

JAMES BROTHERS

The two frontier outlaws Frank and Jesse James have enjoyed legendary status as modern-day Robin Hoods who stole from the rich and gave to the poor. Numerous fanciful movies have painted the James brothers as white knights driven by circumstance and injustice to lead lives of crime. But the James brothers, as portrayed by serious authors and credible researchers, were desperadoes who stole what they refused to earn honestly and killed whoever stood in their way. There is no solid evidence that the two brothers used their booty to benefit anyone but themselves. In other words, Jesse and Frank were little more than self-serving thugs. But the folksingers ramble on: "Oh, the dirty little coward, who shot Mr. Howard, and laid poor Jesse in his grave." It just tugs at your heart, doesn't it?

JAPAN

The picture painted in the minds of most people about Japan is one of crowded cities (wall-to-wall people where everyone owns at least three cameras) surrounded by endless small-plot rice paddies, with picturesque Mount Fuji always in the distance. But this progressive industrial country is not a sea-level land by any means; 75 percent of it is mountainous and a haven for hiking and skiing. Visitors to the green and lush countryside, however, find another experience—a not-so heavenly smell, emanating from the country's thousands of human-waste ("night soil") storage pits used to fertilize their quilted croplands.

JELL-O
Contrary to common belief, the slippery congealed dessert called Jell-O is not the generic product itself, only the trade name given it by its manufacturer. Such a product, manufactured by several food companies, is actually a gelatin.

JELLYFISH
There are two important reasons why the so-called jellyfish are not really fish, but animals: Fish have backbones, making them vertebrates; the jellies have no backbones. Also, fish are three-layered—an inner endoderm, an outer ectoderm, and a middle layer connecting the two. Jellies lack a middle layer, but do have an inner jellylike substance from which they derive their name and which gives them buoyancy. And by the way, the graceful medusa is not the only species in the great seas, there are over two hundred—and counting. Nor do they all look alike. Some jellies carry their own umbrella and have a nasty habit of stinging things, while others appear as cilia-lined combs who leave the stinging to their cankered cousins.

JESUS CLEARING THE TEMPLE
The New Testament of the Holy Bible attests to Jesus clearing the temple (his Father's house) by expelling the money-changers, merchants, and livestock, upsetting furniture, and generally making life miserable for the sacrilegious scalawags therein. This was accomplished during the

Passover celebration wherein the Savior began his public ministry. (See John 2:15.) But, contrary to common understanding, there were actually two temple cleansings. From Matthew 21:12, we learn that Jesus again cleared the temple after his triumphal entry into Jerusalem, which act signified the end of his ministry. "And when he was come into Jerusalem, all the city was moved, saying, Who is this? And the multitude said, This is Jesus the prophet of Nazareth of Galilee. And Jesus went into the temple of God, and cast out all them that sold and bought in the temple, and overthrew the tables of the moneychangers, and the seats of them that sold doves."

JESUS THE CHRIST

Many hold the view that the full name of the son of Mary was Jesus Christ, but according to the Bible, he had but *one* name—Jesus. This, of course, was consistent with the naming of most people in that day; personal identification by surnames didn't come about for many centuries after Jesus' time. The name Christ is a *title*, meaning "The Anointed One"; it is not a surname. The more correct use of his name, then, would be *Jesus the Christ*. This clarification is well illustrated in the book by the same name—*Jesus the Christ* by James E. Talmage.

JIHAD (Holy War)

Because of the social strife that has been manifest in the Middle East during the last few decades, the Arabic word *jihad* has become a familiar part of the American vocabulary. Non-Islamic people generally refer to a jihad as a *Moslem holy war*, but such is not entirely the case. While it is true that the early use of the term meant a religious duty imposed on Moslems to spread Islam by waging war, the modern interpretation has to do more with making war with one's inner self. Thus the word more correctly means to struggle or to make an effort on behalf of oneself. In the recent context of the word, war is sanctioned only as a defensive measure in order to preserve the faith.

JOAN OF ARC

History books are replete with the incredible feat undertaken by the charismatic nineteen-year-old French lass who led the resistance to the English and Burgundians in the second period of the Hundred Years' War—the greatest national heroine of France. So far, so good, but she was *not* French. She was directed, by Michael the archangel, only to "go, to France if you must." Joan was actually from Lorraine, an independent territory ruled by a duke at the time. It did not become a part of France until the middle of the eighteenth century.

JONAH SWALLOWED BY A WHALE

The fact that a large whale is the only sea creature big enough to swallow a man is probably the reason for the mistaken notion people have concerning the biblical Jonah/whale story. But, alas, the Bible only says that poor Jonah was swallowed by a "large fish." And, as any schoolchild knows, whales are not fish but mammals. Big fish, big stories!

JONES, Bobby

There are few people who wouldn't agree that the immortal Bobby Jones was the greatest professional golfer of all time. Anyone open for bets? Who could win the famous "Grand Slam" and not be worthy of such an honor, a feat that entailed winning the U.S. Open, the British Open, the U.S. Amateur, and the British Amateur tournaments, all of which Jones won in 1930. Impressive, yes! But if you bet on him as being the greatest *professional* golfer, you would lose the bet. Bobby Jones regarded golf strictly as a "gentleman's game" and never turned professional.

JOSHUA CROSSING THE JORDAN RIVER

Few people have not heard of the great Red Sea epoch (thanks to Cecil B. deMille's movie *The Ten Commandments*) wherein Moses stretched forth his hand and petitioned the Lord to part the waters, allowing the Israelites to cross over a wind-dried Red Sea leading to the promised land. But few are aware that God performed the same miracle for three other prophets. Joshua 3:7 tells us that Joshua led the Israelites over the river Jordan: "And the Lord said unto Joshua, this day will I begin to magnify thee in the sight of all Israel, that they may know that as I was with Moses so I will be with thee." Verses 16 and 17 elaborate: "The waters which came down from above stood and rose up above an heap very far from the city Adam, that is beside Zaretan. And those that came down toward the sea of the plain, even the Salt Sea, failed, and were cut off, and the people passed over right against Jericho. And the priests that bare the ark of the covenant of the Lord stood firm on dry ground in the midst of Jordan, and all the Israelites passed over on dry ground until all the people were passed clean over Jordan." Dry-river crossings were also made by the prophets Elijah and Elisha. "And Elijah took his mantle, and wrapped it together, and smote the waters, and they were divided hither and thither so that they too went over on dry ground" (II Kings 2:8). Elisha's experience was similar. "And he took the mantle of Elijah that fell from him, and smote the waters, and said, where is the Lord God of Elijah? And when he also had smitten the waters, they parted hither and thither: and Elisha went over." II Kings 2:13,14

JUGULAR VEIN

Doctors, of course, won't be astonished at this mini-course on anatomy, but many people become a little juggled when talking about the so-called jugular vein. To them it is perceived as being a *single* vessel in which blood is carried from the head and neck to the heart. More careful study reveals there are actually two jugular veins on each side of the head—the external and internal jugulars, with even more tributary jugular veins flowing into those main vessels. The external vein lies close to the surface and carries blood from the outside parts of the cranium, the neck, and the deep tissues of the face to the heart. The internal vein is much larger and carries blood from the interior of the skull. It is this larger *internal* jugular that is generally regarded as "the" jugular vein. So if you hear someone remark "go for the jugular," you may want to inquire as to which jugular they're referring to. Also, the word is often misspelled "juggler."

KEYBOARDS, Piano and Organ
As much as we want to keep our pianos and organs designed as they presently are, the early keyboards of those instruments weren't always configured as they are at present; they were in reverse order, with black keys for the lower row and white keys for the accidentals.

KILLER BEES
Predaceous African killer bees are reportedly spreading terror in the minds of Americans who read of the oncoming swarms moving into the Gulf Coast states, supposedly attacking and killing children and animals. But, say the experts, don't buy killer bee insurance yet, it's pure science fiction.

Killer bees sell newspapers but they don't kill people—at least not many people. The folks at the U.S. Agriculture Department's Honey-Bee Breeding, Genetics and Physiology Laboratory at Louisiana State University see a much less ferocious bee winging toward our borders. In fact, the killer bees they know can only be differentiated from their kissing cousins, the European honeybees, by minute measurements and genetic tests; they definitely don't merit their bad press. Although they pose *some* problems, say the bee watchers, they're a more defensive insect than offensive, with a propensity for protecting their colonies at the slightest disturbance. People will occasionally be stung to death by them when they arrive, but, say the experts, sting-sensitive people also get stung to death each year by the gentler European bees, hornets, and yellow jackets. People die because one-half of 1 percent of us are allergic to bee stings. According to the Honey-Bee Lab people, it is expected that fewer people will die from Africanized bee stings than from lightning strikes. Moreover, even our own European honeybees don't escape the rogue role; they too are said to be aggressive, cantankerous, unpredictable, and a host of other uncomplimentary nasties. But, according to A. I. Root's findings outlined in his book *ABC & XYZ of Bee Culture,* bees are "the pleasantest, most sociable, most genial, and best natured little beings that are met in all animated creation, when they are understood." So perhaps we can say they "buzz softly, and carry a big sting"! One more buzzy insight: Despite the reputation bees have for round-the-clock toil, some of them are notorious little thugs who will rob another worker's hard-earned honey any chance they get. And that's remarkably close to the behavior of us humans!

KILLER WHALES

The lovable panda-looking killer whale who puts on his splashy shows for the tourists at Sea World has been demeaned in at least two ways: First, he is not a menacing killer as the name suggests. Monsieur Orca admits to being a predator who takes his place in the food chain, but his munching on marine life is only his way of making an honest living. He doesn't find humans to be particularly tasty, so he leaves them alone; he even bends to their will. And second, whoever thought to name the big guy killer whale did him a disservice at the outset because he is not a whale but a species of dolphin, a member of the family Delphinidae.

KOALA BEARS
Koala bears are not really bears at all, but belong to the family of arboreal marsupials—the "pouchy" crowd that includes Australian kangaroos, wombats, bandicoots, and Tasmanian wolves. The opossum is the only marsupial that lives in the United States. We can only speculate as to how it hitchhiked all the way over to the New World!

KREMLIN
The Kremlin is not just *one building*, or just one Kremlin in one city, but several, the largest one being in Moscow. The capital cities of Pskov, Novgorod, Smolensk, Mostov, Suzdal, Yaroslavl, Vladimir, and Nizhni Novgorod were all built around old kremlins. These walled, triangular fortresses, or citadels, contain a bewildering array of complex buildings including cathedrals, palaces for princes and bishops, governmental offices, and munitions stores. The Moscow Kremlin, initially built of wood but later converted to brick in the fourteenth century, was largely a work of Italian architects, including the Grand Palace designed by baroque architect Rastrelli. Though the kremlins were built as fortresses with moats, ramparts, towers, and battlements, their principal use was not so much for military purposes, but for civic government.

L

LAND OWNERSHIP

We all like to think we *own* the land we stand on and which has been registered in our name. But contrary to popular thought, it is not possible for a person to *own* land; it can only be deeded to him. That's probably due to the fact that land is not removable. (How deep a hole would one have to dig to enable him to say, "I moved my entire land to another location"?)

LASER SURGERY

Patients often marvel at the marvelous laser technology used by surgeons today in medical procedures, but their confidence in their practitioner may wane somewhat if they were to learn there are no certification requirements established to assure that Dr. X is really competent in the use of those lasers.

LAWSUITS

Each day our nation's municipal, state, and federal courts adjudicate approximately 60,000 new lawsuits, making America the most litigious society in the world. "The way to handle the miscreants is to take 'em to court!" Right? Sometimes, but most of the time, no! Court records show that out of that large number of civil lawsuits filed for adjudication, 95 percent are either dropped, thrown out of court, or settled between the contending parties—another way to say "the hassle wasn't worth it!" In fact, a large percent of civil suits result in the litigants coming off *worse* financially than before.

LEAD PENCILS

Simply put, the indispensible lead pencil we've been writing with since the clay tablets of Moses is not made out of lead at all but is a mixture of graphite and clay. The *amount* of clay determines the hardness; the more clay added, the harder the pencil. On the other hand, to say mankind has *never* used real lead for pencils is also erroneous, because the ancient Egyptians and Romans had pencils that were actually made of lead. Ever since about 1500 A.D., however, graphite has been used because it is softer and makes a much darker mark than does lead. So, perhaps we'd better get the lead out!

LEMMINGS

Fiction writers and docu-filmmakers (*White Wilderness,* 1958) have given the skittish little Arctic lemming a bizarre propensity it doesn't really have—that of committing suicide. In truth the genes of lemmings are not programmed for self-annihilation any more than any other animal's. What really happens is that every several years these prolific and peripatetic rodents breed themselves into overcrowded oblivion, sometimes mushrooming their numbers to upward of 100 million, as was the case in Hardanger, Norway, in 1975. The result is that the libidinous little fellows crowd each other into zones of danger, including rivers, lakes, and sea cliffs, the latter being the mythmakers' choice of where the supposed death plunges occur. Lemming expert Arne Semb-Johansson of Oslo University infers that given their large numbers, many lemmings are bound to overshoot the land and somersault down into the killing waters, but their plunge is not intentional, only unfortunate.

LIGER/TIGON

What do we get when we cross a male lion with a female tiger? A "liger," of course. That's not entirely a revelation to many people, but what is supposed by most of us is that such two-for-one aberrations are found in the wild. They are not!

Such animals are hybrids—creatures of captive breeding. A liger in reverse is a "tigon"—the animal that comes when a female lion is romanced by a male tiger. It, too, comes from hybridization. Come to think of it—the tiger and lion come from two different parts of the world, so any kind of chance rendezvous would be out of the question, wouldn't it?

LIGHT BULB

Thomas Edison, though the versatile genius he was, never invented the light bulb, as most people are wont to believe (really wont, in his case). Inventors from France, Russia, and England all had crude, inchoate electrical arc light bulbs years before Edison's time. Mr. Edison's forte was perfecting the existing technology by using a filament of carbonized thread. Ah, yes! We can take the light bulb from Edison but we can't take Edison from the light bulb. Or something like that!

LIGHTNING

All of us know that lightning booms out of nasty-tempered thunderstorms, but few realize it can occur during sand-storms, during snowstorms, during volcanic eruptions, alongside fireballs created by nuclear explosions, and even out of the clear blue sky—"like a bolt out of the blue"! It happens! Perhaps you may remember how fascinated you were with the lightning experiment created (on a de-lightfully sunny day) in your high school physics lab.

LIGHTNING NEVER STRIKES THE SAME PLACE TWICE

It's anybody's guess as to where this baseless notion origi-nated, but it is credence-poor and deserves no further refuting than the fact that New York's Empire State Building gets zapped approximately twenty-three times ever year. This observation wasn't made by people standing in the street gawking up at the tower at just the right moment, but is the result of a ten-year scientific study (1935-41, 1947-49) by the General Electric Company. Another part of the lightning myth is that it always strikes the *tallest* object. Not so! Lightning is no respecter of heights. If lightning always struck the tallest object in town, anything below that level would be spared, and that just doesn't square with the facts.

LINCOLN AND SLAVERY

As is the case with many notables, history sometimes endows them with undeserved accomplishments or notoriety. An example relates to the slave question during Lincoln's administration. Statements from his inaugural address come to mind, wherein he expressly stated he had no wish to interfere with slavery where it already existed. The fact is, during the early months of the Civil War, Lincoln held that he was fighting *not to free the slaves* but to *save the Union.* So, to a large extent, it was the war that was the catalyst for the movement toward an emancipation of the slave population, inasmuch as emancipation was to influence European opinion toward the Northern cause, deprive the Confederates of their productive labor force, and add much-needed recruits to the federal armies. So Lincoln issued a preliminary proclamation promising to free all slaves in Rebel territories who refused to return to the Union. Only when the Confederates remained obdurate did he issue the final proclamation of emancipation. Also, in the final analysis, the proclamation actually freed very few slaves, as most of them elected to remain loyal to their masters after all. So, as to Lincoln significantly freeing the slaves, that's a bit mythy inasmuch as the complete abolition of slavery in the United States wasn't achieved until the Thirteenth Amendment became law throughout the nation, nearly three years later on December 18, 1865.

LIQUIDS ARE INCOMPRESSIBLE?

Most of us are aware that gasses can be easily compressed, resulting in a corresponding increase in temperature—the harder the squeeze, the hotter the mixture. But most are not aware that liquids can also be compressed. Using modern laboratory equipment, lab workers have been able to compress water down to three-fourths of its original volume.

LOG CABINS

Notwithstanding the many paintings depicting log cabins as being the principal domicile built by our early-arriving settlers to this country, such structures weren't actually introduced until approximately 100 years after the Pilgrims arrived. The housing constructed by the first English colonists was typical of what they had in their native country—frame structures with thatched roofs. Pine trees were not plentiful at that time, and still aren't. It was the Swedes who first built the cozy log-pole bungalow that now so typifies the American frontier (which muddies up the water even further, because the word *bungalow* has its origins in India).

LOUISIANA PURCHASE

The geography or history whiz kids probably won't be titillated with this entry, but all too many Americans are totally unaware of the enormous size of territory the United States acquired from France in our historic Louisiana Purchase of 1803. That chunk of North American real estate wasn't just a small plot of Mississippi mud juxtaposed between two Spanish territories in and around Louisiana. Rather, the famous three-cents-per-acre deal included 828,000 million square miles of land that stretched all the way from the Gulf of Mexico to the Canadian border and west to the Oregon Country. In fact, the purchase doubled the size of the United States. Next to the $5-million crap shoot that resulted in the purchase of Alaska from the gullible Russians, the Louisiana Purchase was indeed America's largest, most important expansionist buyout.

M

McDONALD'S HAMBURGER FRANCHISE

Contrary to given McDonald's lore, the successful fast-food chain was not started by the late Ray Kroc, but was actually the brainstorm of two brothers named McDonald—Maurice and Richard. They first started flipping McBurgers in 1937 in Pasadena, California. Ray Kroc didn't become part of the franchising effort until 1954, after which he bought out the two McDonald brothers and put the famous arches on the American skyline.

McDONALD'S IN RUSSIA

All the hullabaloo about the Muscovites lining up for blocks to buy a Big Mac hamburger at Russia's first McDonald's fast-food outlet in January 1990 clouds the fact that it actually *wasn't* the first McFranchise to be established behind the iron curtain, as most people have assumed. The first McDonald's franchises were in place in Yugoslavia and Hungary several years prior to the one in Moscow. At any rate, bourgeois business in Eastern Europe is booming, and only proves what has always been suspected: If given a choice, Ivan prefers hamburgers over cabbageburgers hands down!

MAGNA CHARTA

The revolutionary freedom document long considered the cornerstone of English liberty, and indeed a landmark victory for liberty in oppressive countries, did not grant democracy to all English people as most people envision it; at least not at first. Freedom doesn't come with the wave of a wand. Though some articles in the charter no longer have any importance, many others helped form the foundation for English democracy. For instance, the principle of "no taxation without representation" is traced back to the charter, as is the Right to Habeas Corpus, the Right to Fair Taxation, and the Right to Justice. These, and other rights were implemented gradually and slowly with the passing of time. Notwithstanding the fact that the charter promised certain rights by King John to his subjects, the real intent, as designed by the scheming baronial aristocracy who forced the king to approve it in 1215, was a self-serving effort to protect the rights of that privileged class of estate-rich barons who objected to the high taxes levied on their properties. Essentially the charter was the culmination of a long struggle between the king and the barons for power, and what they, along with certain high church officials, did for individual freedom changed the course of history forever—the first time anyone had ever limited the absolute power of a king. The charter begins with the dreadfully prototypical greeting found in most legal documents of that time, to wit: "John, by the grace of God, King of England, Lord of Ireland, Duke of Normandy and Aquitaine, and Cof Anjou, to the archbishops, bishops, abbots, earls, barons, justicians, foresters, sheriffs, stewards, servants, and to all his bailiffs and liege subjects, greetings." Indeed the document, conceived and *sealed* (not signed) over seven centuries ago, represents an important slice of the past that allows all of us to breathe more freely today.

MALE MENOPAUSE
Casual office-talk sometimes includes stories about men and their supposed "change of life"—similar to that experienced by women. Might as well drop the subject; no such change takes place! Women experience menopause due to a gradual decline in ovarian activity. Or, put another way, they simply run out of eggs. Apparently, males don't run out of anything

except, perhaps, *desire*. According to the experts, there is no sudden downward shift in reproductive ability or hormonal levels as there is with women. Physiologically, men experience nothing like the female climacteric. Many incidences of children having been fathered by men in their old age prove quite conclusively that the old mustangs are able to produce sperm indefinitely. The average levels of testosterone in aging men decline only gradually, if at all.

MAMMOTHS
True, and to be expected, most people are not paleontologically literate when it comes to animals of the distant past; they assume that the mammoths co-existed with the ancient dinosaurs. They didn't! Actually, mammoths and dinosaurs were separated by a giant yardstick of time— approximately 60 million years. Some frozen fellows have been discovered (intact) in recent times, thawed out, and eaten. Yuk! Nothing quite like a well-seasoned mammothburger!

MARATHON
The grueling Olympic-sanctioned, huff-and-puff spectacle that puts a virtual army of runners on twenty-six miles of the village streets in many cities was, contrary to popular belief, never a part of the original Greek Olympics. The longest race of that day was a mere three miles. Legend has it that an excited Athenian runner named Pheidippides raced back from the plains of Marathon, Greece (a distance of about twenty-six miles to Athens) to report the news of the great Athenian victory over the Persians in 490 B.C. But actually, it wasn't until 1908, during the Olympic games in London, that a point-to-point distance was *officially* determined, being the distance from the royal residents of Windsor Castle to the royal box in the stadium at London, a vantage point that allowed the grandkids of King Edward VII and Queen Alexandra to watch the race begin. It wasn't until 1924 that a

marathon distance of 26 miles, 385 yards was officially standardized by the British Olympic Committee. Another difference between today's Olympics and the early Greek Olympics is that many of the Greek events were conducted in the nude, something that would undoubtedly add to the gate receipts if repeated today.

MASON-DIXON LINE

When most people think of the "Mason-Dixon line" they imagine it as being the prescribed Civil War boundary line that divided all the slaveholding territory of the South from the free territory of the North. But the original Mason-Dixon line was a considerably shorter line, drawn nearly one hundred years before the Civil War began. Actually, it was only a 233-mile, east-west boundary line that separated Maryland from Pennsylvania—hardly long enough to separate the entire North from the South. In the 1700s, a border bicker arose between Pennsylvania and Maryland as a result of the loosely drawn charters of those states. The Penn family laid claim to a hefty parcel of Maryland, and Maryland's Calvert family claimed a big chunk of Pennsylvania, including the city of Philadelphia. So in 1760, the quarreling families agreed to have two English astronomers and surveyors, Charles Mason and Jeremiah Dixon, settle the dispute by establishing a boundary along a precise line of latitude—39 degrees, 43 minutes, 26.3 seconds north latitude. And in 1763, the two chaps began their survey, which they finished on October 18, 1767. In the ensuing years the citizens along the line almost really finished it by copping the stones and using them for headstones and other purposes.

MATH AND GENDER DIFFERENCE

The traditionally held belief that boys are superior to girls in math skills has given the gals unnecessary despair and defeatist complexes, causing many girls to avoid math-related subjects in favor of those believed to be more suitable to their gender expectations. (Even the whiz-bang pocket calculators haven't assuaged their supposed innumeracy.) But the most recent studies, including a 1990 study that tested 4 million students, showed that elementary and middle-school girl students actually scored *higher* in math than did boys. Furthermore, when math performance was measured with *grades* rather than by *standardized test scores,* the sallies showed up the boys even in high school. Other, more vintage studies would seem to contradict the above conclusions, but the more recent the studies, the more narrow the math gender gap seems to be.

MAYFLY
The dainty insect called the mayfly is not really a fly. True flies have only two wings; mayflies have four. Its name is also a misnomer inasmuch as it is common from early spring to late fall. A better name for the fragile "fly" is dayfly, since it doesn't eat and lives for only a few hours, which, of course, only figures!

MENDELSSOHN, FELIX
It would no doubt surprise many urbane and well-bred patrons of the arts to learn they have not allowed the great musical genius Felix Mendelssohn the use of his full name. Upon being baptized in 1822 into the Protestant faith at the behest of his family (especially his uncle Jacob), the young genius was officially give the name *Felix Mendelssohn-Bartholdy,* a name he wasn't particularly nuts about but one he never had annulled. Scan some of the sheet music found in your local music store; it sometimes tells it like it is.

MERCHANT SHIPPING
For many years, the small, West African–coast country of Liberia, with a population just under two million, has boasted the largest single-flag merchant fleet in the world, totaling 38,552,000 gross tons in 1971. But does Liberia

really *own* all those ships. It certainly doesn't *build* them! What's going on here? The simple answer is that Liberia *doesn't* own all those ships! Its fleet consists almost entirely of vessels from other countries whose owners register them in Liberia to avoid the higher taxes many other nations levy on shipping. If you're already aware of that bit of marine trivia, you probably aren't of the next one: At the present time, *Panama* has surpassed Liberia in the fleet business. What we're talking about, then, is not actual vessel ownership; both countries are flags of convenience.

MIDDLE AGES

We often perceive of the Middle Ages as being a *set* period of time, but this time classification is at best superficial. The question can be asked: Middle of what? Modern medievalist scholars spread the period out into three distinguishable parts—the Early Middle Ages (500–1000 A.D.), the High Middle Ages (1000–1300 A.D.), and the Late Middle Ages (1300–1500 A.D.). A thousand years is a sizable spread indeed. So you can take a lot of latitude in your arguments about how long a period the so-called Middle Ages really was!

MILESTONES IN MEDICAL SCIENCE

It is only natural to suppose that most of the knowledge mankind has gained concerning medical science has been accumulated over the long time period from the dawn of civilization to the present day. Fortunately for those living today, such is not the case. With the splitting of the atom, another explosion took place—an exponential surge of development in every segment of scientific endeavor, especially in medical science. The speed at which new medical findings has occurred has been nothing short of electrifying. It should, therefore, be not too surprising to learn that most of what is known today about the human body, its functions and the diseases which act upon it has been learned only in the past forty to fifty years. Moreover, it is expected that future scientific discoveries will be achieved in even shorter time periods.

MINNOWS

Fishermen often use minnows as live bait to catch larger fish. And, of course, all minnows are small, are they not? Not necessarily. The mini minnow is not a minnow because it is small, it is a minnow because it is a member of the carp family, where some of the more than 1,000 species grow to be four feet long—like the homely squawfish, for instance. The young of many large non-carp fish are also referred to as minnows.

MINUTE HAND ON CLOCK

Inasmuch as there are twelve hours on the standard clock, it is wrongly assumed that the minute hand passes the hour hand eleven times during that twelve-hour period—noon to midnight. One needs to quickly rotate the hands of the clock for that full twelve-hour period to prove the fallacy of such an assumption. Actually (not counting the noon hour or the midnight hour), the minute hand only passes the hour hand a total of ten times. It may take you half a day and a bit of "skull scratchin'" to figure why that happens, but it does.

MINUTE WALTZ

Frédéric Chopin's "Minute Waltz" (also known as the "Dog Waltz") cannot be played in one minute as the name suggests. It takes approximately ninety seconds to play this presto waltz, depending on the whims and technique of the performer.

MOCKINGBIRDS

Have you ever seen a mockingbird dive-bomb a cat? They're really better at *harassing animals* than *imitating birds*. Despite the birds' reputation for mischievous mimicry, ornithologists say they're not convinced these gabby mockers actually impersonate other birds at all. Most believe they do not. But what the "catbird" *has* going for him is a seemingly endless repertoire of songs of his own making that occasionally sound like the established song patterns of other birds. Consequently, the little snippet is bound to pick up on a familiar tune chirped out by one of his kindred cousins. Perhaps our imagination has a bearing on how we interpret the mockingbird's songs. At any rate, it isn't the mockingbird's natural inclination to play Rich Little with all the other birds in the neighborhood.

MONEY, EVILS OF

The oft-misquoted admonition given by the Apostle Paul in one of his well-known letters to Timothy puts money in a bad light. It needn't! Paul didn't say "Money is the root of all evil," but that *loving* (or coveting) money was the evil. Verse 6:10 of I Timothy leaves no room for speculation: "For the love of money is the root of all evil: which, while some coveted after, they have erred from the faith, and pierced themselves through with many sorrows." Apparently that means you can keep your eight-figure bank account and still get into the kingdom! Eureka! But pay attention to verse 17: "Charge them that are rich in this world, that they be not highminded, nor trust in uncertain riches, but in the living God, who giveth us richly all things to enjoy."

MONKEYS NEVER FALL OUT OF TREES

The movies and television cameras of the past sixty years or so have given us a seemingly endless potpourri of programs and documentaries on wildlife in the jungles and other areas where monkeys like to monkey around. Noteworthy is that few if any of the agile animals can be seen missing the branches as they gracefully swing from limb to limb. It would seem the saying "Monkeys never fall out of trees" is quite correct. But is it? According to those who are in the monkey business and study their population and behavior, the nimble monkeys *do* have their casualties—an estimated one to five thousand monkeys every year. Most of the monkeys survive their high-wire falls, but many of their comrades are killed as a result of their bad bungee jumping.

MORMON CRICKET

In 1848, a plague of Mormon crickets descended upon the Salt Lake Valley and threatened ruination of the entire year's food crop of the Mormon settlers, were it not for the flocks of gulls that suddenly appeared to devour the noxious insects. The dramatic incident has since become known as the "Mormon Miracle." However, contrary to recorded accounts, the crickets did not descend from the *sky* onto the wheat crops, inasmuch as Mormon crickets are unable to fly. The crickets *do* have wings but they are of no practical use; they simply crawl to locate their food source. Moreover, the Mormon cricket is not really a cricket at all, but belongs to the family of katydids and green grasshoppers.

MOSCOW, RUSSIA

The person who has problems with geography (and that includes more than a few) has Moscow situated somewhere within the continent of Asia. A closer look at a map (printed within the last one hundred years or so) will reveal that Moscow is not in Asia but in Europe.

MOTHER GOOSE

Was there really an old Granny Goose who wrote all those children's nursery rhymes, with illustrations depicting herself as a pencil-nosed, sharp-chinned granny riding on the back of a flying goose? The persistent legend that Mother Goose was an actual Boston woman named Elizabeth Goose is untrue, despite the fact that her grave in Boston's Old Granary Burying Ground is still a tourist attraction. No evidence of a book of rhymes she supposedly wrote in 1719 has ever been found. The first U.S. edition of Mother Goose rhymes was a reprint of the Newberry edition published in 1785 by Isaiah Thomas.

MOTHS
Moths are cousins of the butterfly and often just as colorful, but you might want to forget their beauty if you see one flit out of your clothes closet, because he has just eaten your suit. Or so we suppose! Do moths eat clothing? Actually it does little good to administer the coup de grace with a rolled-up newspaper when you see a moth fly out of your closet, because the damage has already been done. The chomping takes place by the infant-moth wrecking team—the freshly hatched caterpillars working overtime to aspire to adult mothhood.

MOTION PICTURE PROJECTION
The believability of a motion picture film projection truly is in the eye of the beholder, but most people don't understand the relationship between the eye and what it beholdeth. When you and I watch a motion picture being projected on a movie screen we're seeing one of the most powerful optical illusions ever performed. What people seem to be seeing is a continuous, uninterrupted animation taking place. But what is actually taking place (but not seen in the film) is about 130,000 *distinct* and *separate* photographs where the separations are imperceptible. The individual pictures project so rapidly through the projector (one frame at a time), they give the illusion of uninterrupted movement, a principle called "persistence of vision," where one picture (frame) seems to blend into the following frame. But when a film projector is activated there are actually thousands of stops and starts throughout the film—twenty-four each second—so that the projection results in dark spots as well as light spots. In fact, the screen is dark for longer periods than it is light, but such short, dark intervals cannot be discerned.

MOTION PICTURE SPEED

Why did everyone move so fast in those vintage motion pictures, like windup toys at full throttle, like World War I soldiers trying to beat each other to the chow hall, and like the hilarious Keystone Cops running at Mach I to catch the town crooks? Charlie Chaplin movies portray the little tramp jerking and skipping as if his pants were on fire. Why all the speed? Most people are under the impression they must have used faster cameras in those days or that the cameras were sped up. The fact is, those old cameras did run at a different speed than today's cameras, but the speed wasn't *faster*, rather it was *slower*. Cameras in the early days of the industry (especially the silent films) operated at a constant speed of only sixteen frames per second, which when projected on present-day equipment (twenty-four frames per second) gives the illusion that the animation is faster than normal. Conversely, cameras operating at faster than twenty-four frames per second project pictures resulting in slower motion. In other words *slow* camera speed results in *faster* screen animation; *fast* camera speed results in *slower* screen animation.

MOTORS VERSUS ENGINES

The main power train of an automobile is often, but erroneously, referred to as a motor. We hear remarks like "Keep the motor running" or "The motor needs a tune-up," but technically speaking, the power train in an automobile is not a motor but an *engine*. A machine that changes electrical energy into mechanical power to perform some kind of work is a motor; it employs no combustion fuel or steam. An automobile engine, on the other hand, is a mechanism that requires some form of fuel such as gasoline, methane, or numerous other energy sources which are burned (exploded) inside the power train. That's why car engines are referred to as internal-combustion engines. (Who ever heard of an internal-combustion motor?)

MOUNT EVEREST

One wonders why the abominable snowman would ever pick the mighty Himalayan Mount Everest for its abode, considering the staggering height of the mountain. Everest does indeed stretch high above the level of the sea (29,028 feet), but what is generally not known is that the distance *below* sea level is considerably greater than Everest's height. Hold your breath and dive down 35,800 feet and you'll come to the deepest hole on Earth—the Mariana Trench in the Pacific Ocean, 200 miles southwest of Guam. If you were walking on the trench, you would be 6.8 miles below the water level. There is another general misconception about ocean depths: The greater depths are not found in the *middle* of the ocean but close to *mountainous islands* where steep shores plunge sharply down to the bottom of the sea.

MOUNTING A HORSE

Why do horses become skittish when riders try mounting them from the right side? Do those plugs have a right/left-brain problem? Or is it because they're conditioned from the start by riders mounting horses in the conventional way? I suppose so! You've never seen John Wayne swing his left leg over the saddle when he mounts, have you? He'd probably fall off, and that wouldn't reveal his "true grit," would it? Maybe it's because mounting a horse from the left side dates back to medieval times when horsemen carried their swords on their left hip, allowing for a more practical mount. Poking a sword in ticklish ribs will unhorse a rider every time. At any rate, there is no truth to the notion that horses instinctively hate right-side mounters.

MOUTHWASHES

With the many grating TV commercials today giving the hard sell to all those over-the-counter mouthwashes, one would suppose they surely must be helping someone alleviate his bad-breath problem! Right? Perhaps not! Reputable research tells us there is no convincing evidence that any medicated mouthwash used as a part of a daily hygiene regimen has therapeutic advantage over a simple saline solution. Yet the great mouthwash racket continues unabated. Save your money and gargle with salt water, and enjoy the joke about the guy who spent a million dollars getting rid of his halitosis, only to learn that nobody liked him anyway.

MOZART, WOLFGANG AMADEUS

The mystique of the gifted musical genius Mozart may survive as long as the incredible abundance of his compositions are played, but one misconception about his death requires correcting: Some accounts claim he was driven to death by an insanely jealous wife; by cholera, which was widespread in Vienna during that time; by excessive bloodletting leading to heart failure; by pneumonia, or by rheumatic fever, from which he suffered numerous attacks during his youth. Unfortunately, history doesn't convincingly bear out *any cause* considered most likely to have killed young Amadeus. What is certain is that he was buried in a pauper's grave attended only by his gravediggers—a terrible ignominy for one who blessed the world with such a priceless musical legacy!

MUSCLE ACHES AND LINIMENTS

How often have you heard the misleading but reassuring ads that promise deep-muscle relief for your muscular aches and pains? Such promises are specious! Even stupid! The effects of all liniments and balms are only superficial, only skin deep. What these supposed elixirs do is stimulate sensory nerve endings in the skin sufficient to produce *sensations* of heat or cold, which in reality only mask the pain of sore muscles. The application of massage along with the liniment may bring some relief, but the help comes almost completely from the massage. So engage a masseur with strong fat fingers, take a couple of aspirin, and have a nice hot bath before bedtime.

MUSCULAR DYSTROPHY

The inherited disease muscular dystrophy, which causes weakness in the skeletal and heart-muscle tissue, and which medical science has worked so long to eliminate, is thought by most people to be a single disease. But, unfortunately, there are at least forty known strains of muscular dystrophy.

MUSICAL INSTRUMENTS

This unprofound information undoubtedly will not alter the tempo of musical-instrument history, but for the record, when one refers to a trumpet or other brass instrument as having keys, he should be aware that such instruments are activated not by keys but by *valves,* sometimes referred to as pistons.

MYTHS

Of all the words in our language, the word *myth* is probably the most mystifying, confusing, and misunderstood. *Fantasy, fiction, fable,* and *falsehood* are words most people generally use to define myths—Mount Olympus fables and fiction! But myths, to the serious scholar, have far more legitimate beginnings and meanings than what people generally ascribe to them. The dictionary defines a myth as a traditional story of unknown authorship, ostensibly with a historical basis, but serving usually to explain some phenomenon of nature, the origin of man, or the customs, institutions, and religious rites of a people. Between the two extremes of definitions there lies a wide spectrum of interpretation. Myths are accounts with an authority that is *implied* rather than stated. Thus there is probably far more truth woven into the complex fabric of the myth than fiction. What is certain, and undoubtedly consoling to the mythologists, is that they will never be called upon to sift through the mystery and legitimize any events that took place so long ago in the past.

N

NAPOLEON
The redoubtable Bonaparte who crowned himself emperor of France and created an empire that covered most of western and central Europe was not a Frenchman as is generally thought but a Corsican. Born August 15, 1769, at Ajaccio, Corsica, in the Mediterranean Sea to parents of Italian nobility, the "little corporal" received only his military savvy in France, where he was commissioned a second lieutenant at the unusually young age of sixteen. Where he got the idea of stuffing half a fist in his vest is anyone's guess.

NARKS
Call a "nark" an informer, a betrayer, a fink, a snitch, a squeaker, a squealer, a stool pigeon, a tipster, or whatever, but the word *nark* (or *narc*) doesn't necessarily have anything to do with a narcotics officer. Since the increase of activity in the modern drug scene, the word has become associated with drugs, but actually it's an old thieves' slang word borrowed from the gypsy word *nak* ("nose"), from *prakrit nakka*. *Nark* generally means an informer, especially a police informer.

NEAR EAST
We sometimes hear the term "Near East" used when referring to a particular geography in the eastern hemisphere, but the term has apparently fallen on hard times, a victim of language decay. The Near East formerly referred to the lands around the eastern shores of the Mediterranean Sea,

including northeastern Africa, southwestern Asia, and the Balkan Peninsula. But today, especially since World War II, the name has been generally replaced by the term *Middle East*. The Far East, however, is holding its own.

NICKEL(S)

Many people take at face value the name of our U.S. coins. For instance, is the five-cent piece—the nickel—really made out of nickel? Some, but not much! Prior to the 1960s our U.S. coins were made of an alloy that contained a good deal of silver, but this was discontinued when the price of silver rose substantially. So the coiners had to put on their innovative hats and design coins another way—by alloying them. Most of today's coins are a blend of 75 percent copper and twenty five percent nickel, including our so-called five-cent nickel. However, in the past, coins made of nickel have been alloyed with zinc, bronze, brass, and silver. So where do we get off calling our nickel a nickel when other coins are similarly alloyed? Good question! We could just as logically call each of our coins nickels except for the penny. Of course, a nickel made out of pure nickel would be far more intrinsically valuable than five cents, and that just wouldn't work out, would it? And what about nickel silver (or German silver)? How much silver is there in nickel silver? Almost none! This alloy is made up of about 60 percent copper, 25 percent zinc, and 15 percent nickel.

NOBEL PEACE PRIZE

We often hear of a person being the recipient of one of the five Nobel Prizes offered each year by the independent Nobel Foundation. Most people assume they are all awarded by Sweden inasmuch as Alfred Nobel was Swedish. The prestigious Nobel Peace Prize, however, is not awarded by Sweden, but by Norway. The other four (physics, chemistry,

physiology or medicine, and literature) are awarded by
Sweden. Additionally, all five prizes do not have to be given
each year. That determination is left to the discretion of the
Nobel Awards Committee.

"NO PAIN, NO GAIN"

Now there's a fitness fiction that should be banished right
into the jogger's twilight zone. Not only is pain unnecessary
in one's march toward physical fitness, it is usually a sign that
someone is huffing and puffing to the wrong cadence.
Sports-medicine experts tell us that people who exercise
should know that pain and soreness are the body's messages
to the brain telling them to stop overdoing it. Records show
that 95 percent of sports injuries can be traced to poor
training methods—most involving the failure to let the body
heal between workouts. The National Athletic Trainer's
Association, in Greenville, North Carolina, reports that most
pain and soreness in sports are attributable to what its
spokesperson calls the "terrible toos—too much, too fast, too
hard, with too little preparation or warm-up." How about a
slow-down slogan like "If there's pain, it's best to refrain"?

NORTH AMERICA, CENTER OF

The exact center of the North American continent, according to the geography experts, is not a point in the center of
the midwest as many Kansas people suppose, but the little
town of Rugby, North Dakota.

OATS

No question about it, today's American consumer is running full-throttle on oat power. Not that this bit of trivia is going to make much difference in your gastronomical lifestyle, but many people have mistaken ideas about quick-cooking oats as opposed to the old-style cooked cereal. Many suspect the manufacturers to have somehow tampered with the chemistry to speed up the cooking process of the quickies, but actually there is no organic, botanic, or chemical difference between the two except that quick-cooking oats are more finely chopped, allowing them to be cooked in about half the time of the others. Be patient, your regular-sized oats will taste just the same.

OCTANE RATING

The liquid hydrocarbon referred to as *octane* has nothing to do with the potential power of gasoline. It is simply a measure of the ability of a gasoline to resist *knocking* when ignited in a combustion engine. The octane number (or rating) of a gasoline expresses the percentage by volume of isooctane in the isooctane-heptane mixture that corresponds in its knock intensity with that of the gasoline. This formula may be Greek to the car owner, but if the old clunker is pinging it may be a good idea to up the octane ante to a higher-rated gasoline.

ODOMETER

That little widget in your automobile with the slow-moving, ever-increasing mileage numbers tells the driver how far his car has traveled since he bought it off the showroom floor. It's called an odometer, not a speedometer, and it has nothing to do with measuring speed. Most think its invention was concurrent with the development of the automobile, but it wasn't. We'll have to go back, way back, to 1500 B.C., when the noted architect and engineer Vitruvius mounted a large wheel of known circumference in a small frame in much the same fashion as a wheel of a wheelbarrow. When the contraption was hand-pushed along the ground it automatically dropped a pebble into a container at each revolution, giving a measure of the distance traveled. Crude indeed, but it was, in effect, an odometer.

OIL SPILLS

The big oil spill in the waters of Prince William Sound, Alaska, gives rise to this entry on gross misconceptions. Oil spills of the magnitude of the Exxon *Valdez* get into the media almost before the oil squirts out of the pipe, but what the public isn't privy to are the approximately 20,000 spills that take place every year in the United States, its territorial waters, and offshore lands. We're talking about an annual average of about 18 to 20 million gallons of oil spilled each year from pipelines, ships at sea, storage facilities, railroad cars, highway trucks, and sundry other leak sources. (If we plugged up all the leaks we might not have an oil shortage.) According to the Conservation Division of the Wilderness Society in Washington, D.C., 17,000 gallons of oil were spilled during the construction of the Alaskan Pipeline. Of course, much of the country's spillage is really leakage—from pipelines, shoreline refineries, and other ancillary facilities that accompany increased offshore drilling, including corrosion-caused leaks from service station tanks, most of which eventually seep through the soil and poison the groundwater of the neighborhood.

"OLD IRONSIDES"

The oldest commissioned active-duty warship in the world is docked inside Boston Harbor. (This very moment!) Formally it is known as the U.S.S. *Constitution*—the name inscribed along its stern. It is also referred to as "Old Ironsides," the intrepid old warhorse that fought in forty-two sea battles without sustaining a defeat, weathered the elements since 1779 when it was built, and for years has staved off numerous attempts to have it scrapped. So perhaps we ought to honor the gallant frigate by exposing the myth that it was built of iron, as the name implies. Actually it was built with oak—strong and sturdy, with a twenty-one-inch hull that prevented enemy cannonballs from penetrating it. Rumor has it that an English seaman could actually see the big balls bounce off the hull, to which he exclaimed "Huzza! Her sides are made of iron!" Other accounts attribute the exclamation to one of the ship's own crew. Climb aboard, mates, it is fully operational and manned by active navy personnel, who take it out of the harbor for an annual exercise and a well-earned show-off. Today, only about 10 percent of the original ship exists. All the rest has been restored from time to time. But it is the live oak, forming the backbone of the ship, which has kept it together and made it possible for it to be restored and maintained.

OLIVE OIL

On your supermarket shelves you can find olive oil labeled extra-virgin, virgin, fine, and ungraded, which leads consumers to regard the labels as having to do with nutritional differences. But those terms only reflect the manner in which the oil is extracted from the olives. You're going to pay a bit more for the extra-virgin because it is the first-pressed and minimally processed oil, but the nutritional values are the same for each category.

OPEN CASKETS

Despite the fact that the funeral industry's Digger O'Dells have convinced the American public that open-casket "viewing" is the best expression of a family's love and respect for a departed loved one, such practice, contrary to what most people may think, is not a part of the funeral service of any modern country except the United States and Canada. Surviving loved ones have the right to keep the lid shut if they so desire.

OWENS, Jesse

Those of us who turned up our little Philcos during the 1936 Berlin Summer Olympics distinctly remember the commentary of how the infuriated Führer snubbed American speedster Jesse Owens after Owens won his gold medal. There's a problem with that story, however. It isn't true! After the first Olympic day (before Owens ran), Hitler didn't congratulate *any* athlete from *any* country. Undoubtedly becoming bored, he had left the games! Nor did the German people snub Jesse Owens; by his own admission, they gave him the greatest ovation of his career.

P

PALOMINO HORSES

Those golden-colored ponies with the white manes and showy frames are erroneously thought to be a distinct breed like Morgans, Tennessee walkers, Arabians, etc. They are not! Actually, the term *Palomino* refers to a horse of a distinct color, which can appear in almost all horses except Thoroughbreds. Because the palomino is not a distinct breed, a mare and a stallion of this color type often produce a foal of a different color.

PANAMA CANAL

There are several misconceptions concerning the construction and operation of the Panama Canal. One is that the three-step locks were constructed because the ocean on one side of Panama is lower than the ocean on the other side, thereby necessitating ships to be raised or lowered to the level of the other. Since the Pacific Ocean is the same level as the Atlantic Ocean, the reason for the locks is to elevate ships up (eighty-five feet) to the higher level of *Gatun Lake*, the large man-made freshwater lake situated in the middle of the canal waterway. Additionally, most people seem to be unaware of the *direction* of the canal. Because of where the canal is situated, ships entering the canal from the Pacific en route to the Atlantic do not travel *east*, but *west*—more precisely, in a *northwest* direction. Conversely, ships moving in the other direction travel in a southeast direction. Another misconception about the canal's locks is that the contained water is forced in through use of powerful pumps. This is also false! One of the many engineering marvels of the canal is that pumping is accomplished not by machine pumps but by the weight of the water itself, gravity-falling from the higher-elevated Gatun Lake, with each filling of the locks requiring about twenty-six million gallons. And because the canal has to be profitable, *all* objects transiting the canal are charged a toll regardless of size. In 1928, a publicity-seeking adventurer named Halliburton *swam* through the canal and was charged thirty-six cents.

PASTERNAK, Boris

Certainly one would suppose that poet and novelist Boris Pasternak, whose celebrated novel *Doctor Zhivago* won him the 1958 Nobel Prize for Literature, had a literary background, but he did not. His training was in music. Pasternak's father was a cultured Jewish art professor who did portraits of important contemporary artists and philosophers, including Leo Tolstoy and Serge Rachmaninoff. His influence obviously had a bearing on young Boris's decision to study musical theory and composition for six years. Also, his mother, pianist Rosa Kaufman, undoubtedly was a factor in that decision. But the world didn't get a Pasternak symphony or singable sonnets; instead it got a prodigious output of poems, books, and literary translations.

PATIENTS AND THEIR RIGHTS

For the many hospitalized people who have come to assume that their bodies aren't their own when in the care and custody of a hospital (this includes perhaps most people), they should know they have more rights than they may have supposed. In 1972 the American Hospital Association adopted a set of twelve right-to-know resolutions which have come to be known as "The Patient's Bill of Rights." The upshot of the bill is that virtually everything done to, and on behalf of a patient, should rightfully and legally be the decision of the patient. One of the most noteworthy of the resolutions is that patients are entitled to thorough access to their medical records, and if there is a change in physicians, for whatever reason, all patient medical records can and should be promptly transferred to the other physician at the patient's request. Most doctors' eyebrows would elevate to their hairline if patients insisted on such rights, but they don't pay the hospital bill, the patient does.

PATTON, George S.

Despite his celebrity and his many singular military achievements, "Old Blood and Guts," the flamboyant World War II army general, was never a recipient of the honor he wanted most—the Congressional Medal of Honor—which many writers have erroneously attributed to him. The pistol-packing Patton was indeed one of the most colorful military leaders but he was also his own worst enemy. All his accomplishments were offset by reckless and bellicose behavior, a loose tongue, and an overbearing egocentricity, for which he received numerous reprimands.

PAUL, The Apostle

Here we have one of the most complex figures of the New Testament. There is little question that the greatest missionary for Christianity during those initial growth years of the Church was this Roman citizen named Paul of Tarsus. Because Paul was a Jew it is generally assumed that he was a Jewish citizen, but such is not so. Rather, he was a proud *Roman citizen* and preferred his Roman name, Paulus, to his Jewish name, Saul. Despite his secular Roman upbringing, his formal education was Jewish. He had been trained as a rabbi under Gamaliel I, a renowned teacher of the Law. After his Damascus experience, the fact of his citizenship undoubtedly was a factor in his rescue from a threatening mob at Jerusalem, where Lysias, the commander of the Roman garrison, saved him and carried him off as a prisoner. Many people also link Paul with the Nazarene, but notwithstanding his incomparable zeal for the principles espoused by Christ, he never actually met or saw Jesus.

PAVLOV, Ivan

Although the name of Ivan Pavlov has often been associated with the techniques of modern-day brainwashing, there is no evidence to support such a belief, albeit his pooch experiments came close to what might be considered animal brainwashing. Actually Pavlov, the son of a village priest with a philosophical persuasion toward egalitarianism, wasn't interested in changing human behavior at all, and even repudiated Communism because of the kind of "social experiment" he saw in it. Said he: "I would not sacrifice a frog's hind legs."

PENGUINS
Most everybody knows that the little tuxedo-clad penguins are birds, but most people suppose they all are indigenous to the Sub-Antartic. Few are aware that penguins also live in more toasty regions like New Zealand, Brazil, Australia, and the coasts of Africa, and even on the *equator*. The Galápagos penguin finds the tropics off South America a suitable place to live. As to the North Pole, despite beliefs to the contrary, only two of the eighteen species living today call the frozen Arctic home.

PENNSYLVANIA DUTCH
Notwithstanding the name, the people referred to as Pennsylvania Dutch are actually not of Dutch descent, but German. The word *Dutch* is a rendering of the German word *Deutsch,* meaning "German." The so-called Pennsylvania Dutch are descendants of seventeenth and eighteenth-century German settlers, primarily from the Rhineland and South Germany, who settled mainly in eastern Pennsylvania—Berks, Lancaster, Lebanon, Lehigh, Northampton, and York counties. Some immigrants came from the German part of Switzerland, others were French Huguenots. At any rate, none came from the Netherlands. Being slow at acculturation, they cling today to their European traditions, where they emphasize savory cooking and decorative motifs, such as the hex signs painted on their barns.

PERFECT PITCH

Twelve-year-old Rebecca sits at the seven-foot Steinway struggling through an Elgar chanson, accompanied by an equally struggling pianist. Her parents nod approvingly. "She has perfect pitch!" they proudly exclaim. "Well, almost!" says the astute voice teacher. "You see, the pitch of most sounds is actually due to a *blend* of various frequencies. The sounds produced by a musical instrument, a whistle, a siren, or the human voice all have several frequencies at the same time. So the chance of your little prodigy pitching her voice to the so-called perfect spot in the range of sounds would be quite unachievable." In other words, there's really no such thing as true perfect pitch. "But," says the teacher, "Rebecca is making progress!"

PERMAFROST

Despite what is generally believed regarding the makeup of Alaska's vast frozen subfloor called permafrost, it is not made up entirely of frost, or even ice. Permafrost is ground that stays substantially frozen for periods of between two years to thousands of years, and is a conglomerate of many kinds of material—bedrock, gravel, sand, or pure ice. Even so, you probably wouldn't want to build a permanent house on permafrost.

PETRIFIED WOOD

The term "petrified wood" is really a misnomer. The petrification process takes place when mineral water fills the cells of decaying wood and replaces the original wood fibers until the whole log structure has become solid stone. But having gone through that process, it is no longer wood, even though it still shows every detail of the original wood.

PIANO-PLAYING BY EAR

We often hear of someone who supposedly is capable of playing the piano by ear. To begin with, the whole notion of playing "by ear" is not only misleading but even elicits a "measure" of humor (no pun intended)—playing the piano by one's ears would indeed be a play on the imagination. All music consists of chords, rhythm, and melody, which are the elements that give identification to a particular musical work. A pianist must first acquaint himself with these elements of a song in order to be able to interpret them and subsequently give expression to the melody via the keyboard. You can be certain that those pianists who seem to be able to respond to any and all happy-hour requests from salon patrons have *memorized* a lot of songs before they played them by ear.

PIGS

In the 1960s, the disheveled counterculture group of hippies and generally malcontented troglodytes took out their frustrations on the police with the taunt of "pigs." But just as there was little originality in their protestations, neither was there any originality in their use of the abasing term *pigs,* for it was used centuries before our day by the sullen children of Israel against the police authority of the Roman Empire during their period of captivity. And during the Crusades of the thirteenth century, German Emperor Frederick II—the Stupor Mundi, Wonder of the World—called the Christians "infidels and pigs" while addressing an Arab group in a mosque.

PILGRIMS

When we think of all those dedicated Pilgrims sardined aboard the *Mayflower* destined to the New World, we envision a crude ship overladen with oppressed members of the English Separatist Church. But how many actual Pilgrims were aboard the *Mayflower?* According to the most reliable accounts, only two-thirds of the total passengers were Pilgrims, the other one-third were escorts (guards) hired by a London Stock Company to protect the company's interests in financing the pilgrimage to America. Two of these escorts were Miles Standish and John Alden. (Remember them?)

PIZZA PIE
People hooked on pizza love the stringy, cheesy delicacy so much they probably wouldn't be bothered at all if they were to learn that the term *pizza pie* is an exercise in redundancy. The word *pizza* actually stands for *pie*, so, in essence, when a person orders a pizza pie he is ordering a *"pie pie."* Enjoy!

PLASTICS
It is commonly thought that plastic was first extruded out of the industrial furnaces in *our* generational day, but crude plastic was actually a product of the *last* century. Parkesine (later called Xylonite), was first exhibited by the English chemist and inventor Alexander Parkes in 1862. His goop was essentially a nitrocellulose substance softened by vegetable oil and camphor. American John W. Hyatt improved on the Parkes idea and invented celluloid by heating a mixture of nitrocellulose, camphor, and alcohol under pressure to make it pliable for molding. International brains then vectored in on the idea to bring crude plastic up to the present-day state of the art. Now, unfortunately, even keener brains are needed to get rid of the pervasive stuff.

PLASTIC SURGERY
The precise procedure for grafting skin from one area of the body to the other—plastic surgery—is most generally regarded as a modern-day development because of the technology involved and the required training, but such is not the case. Physicians, practitioners, and crafty wizards were performing successful skin grafts (mostly for burns) as early as the sixth century in India and China.

PLO/PALESTINE LIBERATION ORGANIZATION
It is wrongly supposed that the anti-Israel guerrilla organization the Palestine Liberation Organization is a single monolithic organization led by Yasir Arafat, the grizzly guerrilla

with the Ralston-Purina feedbag turban. Actually there are several prominent groups under the PLO umbrella who at times sup at a common terrorist table but who more often than not toss chicken bones at each other over policy. For the most part, Arafat's larger al-Fatah group throws bigger chicken bones, and consequently gets more of the world's attention.

PLUM PUDDING, English
In 1658 the Chevalier d'Arvieux described English plum pudding as "a detestable compound of scraped biscuits of flour, suet, currants, salt, and pepper made into a paste, wrapped in a cloth, and boiled in a pot of broth." Not a word about plums! That's because authentic English plum pudding has no plums. Initially (prior to 1600), plum pudding started as a kind of porridge, a soft gruel or soup, made at first with plums but later with raisins, currants, and spices, especially ginger. These savory scents were stirred into a beef or mutton broth and thickened with brown bread crumbs. It didn't evolve into the celebrated pudding we know today until the late 1600s, when creative Anglo-Saxon cooks gradually began transforming it into the baronial pudding that ushers in Christmas in flaming style.

PLUTO AND NEPTUNE, Orbital Positions
Part of the hickory-stick education received by those who stayed awake during their astronomy classes was memorizing the planets of our solar system with their respective orbits and relative distances from the sun. The good memorizers learned that the plant Pluto is the farthest planet from our sun. However, that textbook information was both correct and incorrect! The reason is, Pluto's peculiar orbit is more oval than that of other planets, and being so, crosses over inside Neptune's orbit. In 1979 Pluto's orbit brought the planet 56 million miles inside Neptune's orbit, where it will stay until 1999. During those twenty years Neptune will

actually be the planet farthest from the sun, not Pluto. After 1999, of course, the two planets will behave themselves by getting back to where they used to be. Interestingly, the two planets were in that crossed-over position during the fly-by of the *Voyager* satellite in August 1989.

PLUTO'S DENSITY
For many years it was believed (by the mature population) that Pluto's mass was more than 90 percent of Earth's. Today's more accurate calculations do a complete flip-flop; it is Earth that has a mass 90 percent greater than Pluto's.

POE, Edgar Allan
To think of Edgar Allan Poe is to think of a man obsessed with the lurid and the macabre—ghouls, caskets, black ravens, and insanity. Albeit Poe's violent temper, hyper-acidity toward his literary peers, and (hic) alcoholism set him up for the venemous quills of biographers, he nevertheless wasn't entirely the Dr. Strangelove that most people perceive him to have been. By far the larger part of his writing (which included comedy, poetry, science fiction, and adventure) did not deal with morbid themes, but blended conventionality, originality, and romantic imagination. Poe was foremost a hard-working writer, editor, publisher, and serious journalist who once dedicated poems to the cadets of the U.S. Military Academy, from which he had been previously dismissed. His vindictive literary associate Rufus Griswold, whom Poe named his literary executor, was responsible for much of the defamation heaped upon this gifted tell-tale writer.

POINSETTIAS
Those brightly colored tropical poinsettias that seem to show up every Christmas season are as misunderstood as they are beautiful. First, they are not really plants, as thought by most people, but *trees*. Myths have existed for many years that poinsettias are extremely toxic. Though their milky sap can

irritate the eyes and sensitive skin, the crimson delights are not bad guys after all. People are naturally fascinated by their brilliant petals, but those aren't the flowers, they are the leaves, called bracts. The true flower parts of the poinsettia are the tiny yellow-green nubs or buttons in the center of the red leaves. But now the biggest misconception—the name itself. Most people call them poinset*tas,* but a closer look at the spelling tells us they're eliminating an important vowel, namely the *i.* The correct pronunciation, then, is poinset*tias.* A final word about their origin: Poinsettias are not indigenous to the United States but were originally cultivated by the Central American Indians. They were later introduced into the United States by our first ambassador to Mexico, Joel Roberts Poinsett, which, of course, figures.

POLLUTION OF THE EARTH

When the average temperature in the world goes up or down a few degrees, we can expect a bit of hype from the media, from scientists, pseudo-scientists, and doomsday prophets, all predicting the worst scenario soon to be thrust upon mankind. Whether it's the greenhouse effect, chemical residues from pesticides, or the dangers of nuclear radiation, the monitions can be expected. But are we "straining at gnats and swallowing camels"? Maybe so! For instance, all the carbon dioxide put into the atmosphere by the entire human race has been estimated to be less than one-fifth of what is spewed out naturally by volcanoes alone. Natural pesticides produced by plants put many times more cancer-causing chemicals into our bodies than all the man-made pesticide residues in the world. The miniscule amount of nuclear radiation created by man pales in the face of that which nature serves up.

PONY EXPRESS

There are many who believe that America's Pony Express mail-delivery system was a *nationalized* U.S. enterprise, but it was not. The government didn't own the nags that were put to the whip, nor were the riders on the federal payroll. Also, many have come to believe this horsing-around mail delivery system failed because it wasn't profitable, but its demise wasn't due to unprofitability but to the advent of the newly installed coast-to-coast telegraph communication system. Aside from its slow, galloping delivery system, the Pony Express, which lasted only eighteen months, served only a relatively small area of the country—the area between St. Joseph, Missouri, and Sacramento, California. In contrast with the telegraph system, which offered instant communication, one-way trips by the Pony Express took up to ten days to complete. Hence it was a matter of sheer expediency that the service be terminated. Needless to say, with all the resources in place, the sponsoring firm of Russell, Majors, and Waddell lost a bundle. It is also a misconception to suppose that the Pony Express was the world's first horse-mail attempt at sending messages to Garcia; horse-mail delivery was in place in Cyrus the Great's Persia (around 540 B.C.) and in Alexander's empire two centuries after that, reaching its fullest development among the nomads of the Asiatic steppes. It also thrived in Outer Mongolia, beginning thousands of years ago and lasting until the 1920s.

POP GOES THE WEASEL

Nursery rhyme lovers have always questioned just what in the world there could be about a weasel that could make it "pop"? Like many dubious children's rhymes that have their origins in Old England, this preposterous poesy has a simple explanation. Nineteenth-century Englanders wouldn't have thought a weasel could explode either, but they *did* know that the crude stitching or sewing devices of that day were called weasels: "A penny for a spool of thread, a penny for a needle, that's the way the money goes, Pop! goes the weasel." Now you know! You cannot pop a weasely weasel!

PORCUPINE
The lumbering rodent with the quiver full of darts often gets credit it doesn't deserve. The truth is, porcupines don't *throw* quills at anyone or anything. An animal or person can be spiked with quills only if it gets close enough to be hit with the porcupine's fast-moving tail, which flips out with uncanny accuracy. The other glaring myth about Mr. Porky has to do with the nature of the quills, which are mistakenly thought to release a poison upon contact. They do not! Serious damage can result, however, if the victim is unable to extract the barbs, resulting in a swelling of the face sufficient to hinder its ability to feed itself.

PORTLAND CEMENT
Because of its name, people often assume that portland cement comes from Portland, Oregon, or Portland, Maine, or from several other cities of that same name. It doesn't. The inventor of this ghostly bonding powder—Joseph Aspdin of England—perfected the basic substance in 1824, naming it because it had the same color as the natural stone quarried on the Isle of Portland, a peninsula on the south coast of Great Britain. Also, most of us are prone to confuse cement with concrete. We speak of cement roads, but those long ribbons of highway aren't cement, they are concrete. Cement is a powdered calcined rock and clay material which is only one of several ingredients that makes up concrete. It serves as the adhesive (or glue) used to harden the concrete.

PRAYING MANTISES EATING EACH OTHER
Cannibalism before copulation on the part of female praying mantises might provide a measure of perverted glee to some people, but studies highlighted in the August 1984 issue of *Animal Behavior* showed that Ms. Mantis sees little point in decapitating her hapless suitor prior to mating. This is not to say that it doesn't sometimes happen, but only in instances of what the article refers to as "an artifact of captivity," wherein

the aggressive females were somehow violated or were not properly fed. In such cases the "decapitator's hunger held priority over its sex needs."

PRECIOUS METALS—Silver, and Copper

Most people are not really expected to know much about precious-metal mining, and they don't. We assume, for instance, that what comes out of silver mines is mostly silver. This notion is far from true. Precious metals are seldom found in isolation as we might think, but are sparsely scattered throughout the ore in relatively minute amounts, requiring expensive refining to achieve separation. In silver mines, lead is the most abundant mineral, which, in many instances, is so thickly veined, it can be scraped with a pocketknife. Copper mines are no exception; their ores usually contain less than 4 percent copper. Furthermore, none of the mined copper is pure, and that found to be nearly pure is rarely found in its natural setting.

PROCTOLOGY DEBUNKS

In no other field do we have more misconceptions and differences of opinion than in the medical field, and proctology is no exception. Most modern-day proctologists generally agree that daily bowel movements aren't—repeat—*aren't* essential to good health and that sitting on the john while you read the entire *Wall Street Journal* doesn't coax out hemorrhoids (although a steep drop in the Dow might do it)! As to frequency of bowel movements, it varies in much the same way that people differ in the amount of sleep required. People are not automatons in their physiological processes, and bowel movement schedules can vary from once daily to weekly, and sometimes longer. Regularity is the key, not frequency. Also contrary to what many have been led to believe, the experts say that cancer does not result from the absorption of toxins that supposedly pass through the colon wall.

PSYCHOSOMATIC ILLNESS

We've all heard the familiar phrase, "It's all in your head," meaning that whatever is supposedly bothering you is not physical, but mental (a psychosomatic illness)—the last thing a beleaguered person wants to hear. The use of the word *psychosomatic,* however, is not only medically improper, in most cases, but misleading and dangerous. Only a simpleton would be inclined to use it when referring to his patients. In those rare cases where a doctor might conclude that something is all in one's head, the proper diagnostic term would be *psychogenic,* which means "originating in the mind." Breaking down the word *psychosomatic* gives us some insight; *Psyche* is the Greek word for the mind; *soma* is the Greek word for the body. The word *psychosomatic,* then, implies an interaction between the mind and the body. The experts tell us nearly every illness has a psychosomatic component, which can be seen as an interaction of biological, social, and psychological factors. Thus the word *psychosomatic* is applied to a broad range of illnesses that include those caused by bacteria or even by mental trauma. Knowing this, you probably feel better already!

PURSUIT OF HAPPINESS

We like to regard our cherished Declaration of Independence as a spontaneous dash of inspiration, once written, never needing to be changed. But there was indeed an important change unknown to most people. The original document did not read "life, liberty and the pursuit of *happiness*", rather it read "life, liberty and the protection of property." Hindsight historians look back on the change as an effort on the part of the founding fathers to divert attention from their own large real estate holdings. We still have a bit of that in politics today, eh?

Q

QUARTER HORSE

The fast and stocky quarter horse is often, but erroneously, thought to be a quarter (or more) of other breeds of horses. It isn't! Rather, it's an established breed in itself, having originated in England and having been bred for speed and handling in the United States. Its name comes from its ability to run a blistering quarter-mile race—at that shorter distance it is considerably faster than long-distance thoroughbred racehorses.

QUICKSAND

More than a few movies have featured hapless humans being sucked into that unmerciful muck called *quicksand*—sinking and sorrowing like a struggling pig being ingested by a python. Such scenes increase the thrill index of the theatergoer, but the superfine, supersaturated sand that supposedly does that is no such villain. Quicksand becomes quicksand only when there is a sufficient underground water source to enable the sand above to be suspended, or to become less dense. Such sand is usually found on sandbars, on the bottom of streams, or on the sand flats along seacoasts. But because of quicksand's particular density and high specific gravity, objects such as flailing human bodies, for instance, are not able to fully sink below the surface. So with a little patience, and with the help of a rescuer and a rope, the quicksand need not be one's final burial place

QUOTATIONS

In defense of those who seemingly use another's ideas or words, it isn't always easy to determine when one has borrowed golden nuggets from someone else's mother lode. The following are a few *misquotations* you may want to rearrange in your mind:

a. "Government of the People, by the People, for the People." Did Abraham Lincoln really originate that famous "people" phrase contained in his Gettysburg Address? Probably not! At least four other early political figures used such, or similar, terminology—John Adams in 1798, John Marshall in 1819, Daniel Webster in 1830, and the Rev. Theodore Parker, who, speaking at a Boston antislavery meeting in 1858, used the phrase three separate times. In a July speech in Boston he declared, "Democracy is self-government, over all the people, for all the people, by all the people." William Henry Herndon, the law partner of Abraham Lincoln, states in his *Life of Lincoln,* that Lincoln had a copy of Parker's sermon and marked that particular passage.

b. "Go west, young man, go west." Horace Greeley didn't originate that quote; it came from John B. Soule writing in the *Terre Haute Express* in 1851.

c. "Iron curtain." Journalists, more often than not, attribute to Sir Winston Churchill a quotation he didn't actually originate, namely, the one about the "iron curtain." The gifted communicator and orator did indeed use such a term in a speech given March 5, 1946, at Fulton, Missouri, but Germany's phooey peddler, Joseph Goebbels, used it a year earlier in an article called "The Year 2000." In the article Goebbels told the occupied countries that if Germany did not destroy the Soviet Union, an "iron curtain" would descend over all of Europe, separating its ancient and glorious civilization from the rest of the world. Other iron curtain wordsmiths who used the term were George Crile, Vasily

Rozanov, and Ethel Snowden, who, as early as 1920, wrote: "We were behind the 'iron curtain' at last!"

d. "Millions for defense, but not a cent for tribute." Usually that quotation is attributed to Charles Cotesworth Pinckney as being his response to Talleyrand's bribe to stop the attacks on American shipping. But it was actually uttered by legislator Robert Goodloe Harper. As it turned out, the United States eventually *did* pay the Barbary pirates the tribute money they demanded to secure the release of American citizens held in captivity.

e. "Old soldiers never die, they just fade away." It was a brilliant and memorable speech the erudite General Douglas MacArthur made in April 1951, before a joint meeting of Congress, when he said "Old soldiers never die, they just fade away." But, by his own admission, the retiring general didn't originate that sentiment; it dates back to World War I and is part of the lyrics of an old English military ballad.

f. "Patriotism is the last refuge of a scoundrel." England's Samuel Johnson, one of the most outstanding figures of English eighteenth-century life and letters, said "Patriotism is the last refuge of a scoundrel." This misunderstood aphorism has drawn the ire of patriots for over two hundred years, but Johnson wasn't denigrating patriotism, he was denouncing scoundrels who would slander a patriot's name.

g. "That government is best which governs least." This quotation is more often than not attributed to Thomas Jefferson but, in fact, it came from Henry David Thoreau. Thoreau used that sentiment as a "motto," and placed it in quotation marks.

h. "We have awakened a sleeping giant." There is no evidence of that statement ever being made by Admiral Isoroku Yamamoto, who commanded the Japanese combined fleet at the time of the attack on Pearl Harbor in 1941. It actually originated with Napoleon, who was referring to China.

i. "Never give a sucker an even break." We can just imagine W. C. Fields mouthing that acrid remark about the unlucky losers he often chided, but Fields didn't actually say it, the writer Wilson Mizner did—he was a gambling man.

j. "Elementary, my dear Watson," If Sir Arthur Conan Doyle put that saying in any of his writings it is well hidden. One can, however, find it in a 1929 movie entitled *The Return of Sherlock Holmes.*

R

RABIES IN DOGS

Mention the word *rabies* and most likely it will trigger a vision of frothy-mouthed mutts running around the neighborhood in pursuit of a pair of denim britches. But dogs are involved in only 4 percent of all the animal-bite-contributed rabies reported each year. The other 96 percent of rabies-bite cases come from raccoons, skunks, bats, and humans. An average year for dog bites involving rabies is only about 100 cases. Following dogs and cats, human bites account for 1 to 15 percent of all recorded cases in America. So maybe we should be looking for people biting dogs!

RACCOONS WASHING THEIR FOOD

Are raccoons really all that fussy about eating clean food? Out of water they don't clean their food, so why are they seemingly fastidious when in a stream? Actually, raccoons only *appear* to be washing their food, nervously turning over rocks and sand to catch whatever variety of crustaceans their nimble hands can find. Check it out! The next time you see a raccoon pilfer a goodie from your back porch, check to see if it runs over to the faucet to clean off the dirt!

RACEHORSE STAMINA

If you're much into horse racing, you may have noticed how winning horses seem to pick up speed as they approach the finish line. Most of the frenzied crowd watching the race believe it's because the front-runner is actually *moving ahead* of the other horse, i.e., it is accelerating. In truth it's only because the other animals are getting pooped sooner. Consider the incredible performance of the great Triple Crown thoroughbred Secretariat, who led the field by more than thirty lengths at the Belmont Stakes in 1973. Secretariat was indeed an incredible running machine, but despite his stamina, he wasn't accelerating as he approached the finish line; he, too, was winding down, but at a slower rate than the others.

RADIO

Throughout much of the first half of the present century, radio was king—the indispensable source of news and entertainment. With the advent of television, most people think radio has dropped from king to prince. Not so! At least, not in terms of sales! On the contrary! Audio communication has not declined, rather it has *increased*. More radios are sold per capita today than ever before.

RADIOCARBON DATING

The method of estimating the age of organic material by measuring its content of carbon 14 radioactivity is known as radiocarbon dating, a system many people wrongly suppose can determine the age of *all* organic matter regardless of how old it is. The fact is, radiocarbon dating is useful only for objects of up to about 70,000 years of age—a mere dot of time when considering how old the earth is. This, of course, would exclude all those old lizards and their prehistoric kindred who lived millions of years ago, and whose skeletal forms are imprinted in the timeless rocks for the whole world to marvel at. Newer forms of radiometric dating, however, can now pick up the really old stuff.

RALEIGH, Sir Walter

The tobacco cans imprinted with the picture of Sir Walter Raleigh have done much to make the man's name well known and sell tons of tobacco leaves. But there's a myth about Raleigh's role in the promotion of that foul substance to England. It wasn't to England that Raleigh initially introduced the aromatic weed, as is generally thought, rather it was first introduced to Spain and France, then finally to England, where Sir Francis Drake promoted it in the 1580s. Notwithstanding Raleigh's role in popularizing tobacco in England, King James I actually banned the stuff, describing it as "loathesome to the eye, hateful to the nose, harmfull to the braine, dangerous to the Lungs, and in the blacke stinking fume thereof, neerest resembling the horrible Stigian smoke of the pit that is bottomlesse."

RED BARON

Red-Baronmania has continued to sweep the country since World War I, fueled by the movies, books, and a comic-strip doggie named Snoopy. But we have to forget about most of those legendary dogfights that pitted Fokkers and Pfalzes against Sopwith Camels and Spads, because it didn't happen quite that way. In fact, the famed "Fokker Scourge" operation lasted only about eight months, and most of the flying done by the Sopwith Camel was for deadly trench strafing. As for the Red Baron's eighty kills, history reveals they weren't accomplished through dogfights but through stealth and surprise. According to the curators at the Smithsonian Institution, the German Pfalz D.XII logged more hours flying in Hollywood aviation films than it did against enemy aircraft. Older-generation movie buffs may remember the 1930 version of *The Dawn Patrol* showing the fighter with a fictitious red color scheme and a skull and crossbones painted on the fuselage. Aviation buff Howard Hughes then bought the relic to produce the film *Hell's Angels,* and finally, it starred in *Men with Wings.* The Smithsonian people refer to the fighter's wartime involvement as "obscure" at best.

RED SPIDER
The little red varmint that kills off your pretty evergreens every year, and which seems to ignore the poison that's supposed to kill it, is not really a spider at all. Rather, it is a tick, or what is often referred to as a mite. Prevention is usually best to keep the mighty mite under control because by the time you find it and clobber it, your evergreen is no longer green.

RED SQUARE
Even though Red Square was the location of the annual Russian parades commemorating May Day and the October Revolution, its name is not derived from Communism. This ceremonial center, the historic hub of Moscow, was named *prior* to the revolution. The name Red Square derives from the old Russian word for "beautiful."

RELATIVE HUMIDITY
It is a common misunderstanding that relative humidity is a constant indicator of the amount of water in a given amount of air at a given moment. But humidity doesn't check out that easily. A relative humidity reading indicates how much moisture the air can hold at its *current* temperature. Therefore, a relative humidity of, say, 80 percent in the hot month of July, is not the same as a relative humidity of 80 percent in

the cold month of December. The 80 percent summer reading would be more moist than the December 80-percent reading. This is because warm air holds more water vapor than cooler air. It really is relative after all!

RELIGION ON THE DECLINE IN THE UNITED STATES?

The much-talked-about decline of religion in the United States and the consequent secularization of American society is a myth. On the contrary! America's basic religious beliefs, church membership, and church attendance have changed almost not at all since the 1930s. Those are the conclusions of two studies published in 1989—one by pollster George Gallup, Jr., and journalist Jim Castelli, the other by Roman Catholic sociologist, priest, and novelist Andrew Greeley. According to Gallup and Castelli's book, *The People's Religion: American Faith in the 90's,* 94 percent of Americans believe in God. Nine in ten Americans pray. Eight in ten Americans believe that God still works miracles, and seven in ten Americans believe in life after death. The Gallup data on church attendance reveals that little has changed in the past fifty years. In 1937, 41 percent of Americans polled said they attended church in a typical week. In 1988, 42 percent of Americans said they did. Additionally, church membership, which was 73 percent in 1937, stayed relatively stable at 65 percent or more during the 1980s. Apparently Beelzebub isn't getting many converts in America!

REVERE, Paul

Thanks to Henry Wadsworth Longfellow's poem "Paul Revere's Ride," an important piece of Colonial America's history has been illuminated for us. However, the poetic version of the 1775 saga was both incomplete and inaccurate; some important players were omitted. What about fellow patriots William Dawes and Dr. Samuel Prescott—two deserving town criers getting no respect? Everyone knows about Revere's gallop through the Boston countryside alerting the villagers: "The British are coming! The British are coming!" (Some historians believe he said, "The regulars are about! The regulars are about!") So let's put this event in proper perspective with a short narrative: Word had it that Lieutenant Colonel Francis Smith, commander of the British redcoat regulars, was to dispatch 700 troops to Concord for the purpose of destroying patriot military supplies stored in anticipation of an impending rebellion. The expedition boarded waiting boats at the foot of the Boston Common and rowed across the river to Cambridge. From there they were to march on Lexington and Concord. Now enter the two patriots Paul Revere and William Dawes, who take slightly different routes to warn the villagers along the way to Lexington and Concord concerning the enemy's tactical movement. (In addition to their countryside alarm the two patriots are also anxious to warn the snoozing Samuel Adams and John Hancock at Lexington of the redcoat troop movement.) Both men reach Lexington and warn Adams and Hancock as planned, but this is the end of the trail for those two patriots, who are interdicted at that point by the British in Lexington. Now enter a third patriot who, by happenstance, was met by Revere and Dawes—Dr. Samuel Prescott. It was Prescott who spurred his steed on from Lexington, alarming all the villagers en route to Concord. So what about this fellow Longfellow and his schoolboy poem? Simply put, Paul Revere never made it to Concord.

> It was two by the village clock,
> When he came to the bridge in Concord town.
> He heard the bleating of the flock,
> And the twitter of birds among the trees,
> And felt the breath of the morning breeze
> Blowing over the meadows brown.
> And one was safe and asleep in his bed

Who at the bridge would be first to fall,
Who that day would be lying dead
Pierced by a British musket-ball.

RICKSHAWS

Certainly nothing could be more Oriental than the muscle-powered rickshaws that were, to the Orient, like the passenger pigeon was to North America—all over the darn place!—a contraption no more than one generation removed from the discovery of the wheel. So it would seem! It would seem that the flippin' idea was decidedly an Oriental invention. Wrong, for two reasons: First, it was not invented by the Asians, but by an American Baptist minister. And it wasn't invented eons ago, but closer to the year 1869, which in Oriental terms is almost modern state of the art. Today, however, the rickshaws have largely been replaced by pedicabs, which look and smell like rickshaws, but are ambulated by sprocket power.

RIGHT-OF-WAY RULE/INTERSECTIONS

If you haven't taken a driver's written test lately, or are not familiar with right-of-way rules, you may be under the impression that when two vehicles approach an uncontrolled intersection at the same time, the driver on the right has the right-of-way. (Isn't that what *right-of-way* means?) Not so! The law doesn't establish who *has* the right of way, rather it establishes who *doesn't* have the right of way (or who must *yield* the right of way). This makes sense because it puts the focus on caution and safety, not on rights. You may want to familiarize yourself with this tidbit of traffic trivia; it may help you pass your next frustrating driver's test.

RING AROUND A ROSY

The dopey little nursery rhyme that has all the children in the circle falling down has a questionable provenance. It supposedly dates back to the time of the Black Plague, wherein plague victims experienced a rose-colored sore within a similarly colored circle—the initial manifestation of the affliction. The part about the "pocket full of posies" is even more grotesque, supposedly relating to the flowers stuffed into the afflicted person's clothing to counteract the strong stench emanating from the sore. Finery! But this fickle fable has problems! Assiduous "rosy" researchers point out that neither the rhyme itself nor the game it relates to has anything to do with the terrible plague of fifteenth-century England. That's because the earliest report of the rhyme dates back only until about the mid-nineteenth century, and the plague legend can be traced only to the middle of the present century. Still, the legend lives on—more distended and absurd with each retelling.

ROME

The familiar saying "Rome wasn't built in a day" should also include the dictum that Rome wasn't built by the Romans at all. It was actually built by the Etruscans, an effete civilization that dominated central Italy for more than 500 years before being taken over by the superior might of the Roman Empire. We're also going to have to take away some other things from those Promethean Romans, such as Roman numerals, for instance; they too were of Etruscan origin. And while we're at it, we should credit those sensuous Etruscans for bringing us the banquet, the toga, the keystone arch, and water conduits, in addition to being among the first to cultivate grapes and olives. And finally, just one more benign swipe at the Roman Empire, which prided itself on its ingenious system of highways: The earliest roads in Europe were the "Amber Routes," used between 1900 and 300 B.C. by Etruscan and Greek traders who transported amber and tin from the north of Europe to points on the Mediterranean and Adriatic.

ROOSEVELT, Theodore

Poor Teddy Roosevelt! He was the youngest person ever to hold the office of President of the United States, but no one believes it. They even named the teddy bear after him, but not because of his young age. Alas, the young-president image unjustifiably goes to John F. Kennedy. While it is true that Kennedy was the youngest *elected* President, at age forty-three, Teddy Roosevelt was only forty-two when he became President upon the death of William McKinley. The confusion comes from the fact that although Roosevelt had already been in the White House for three years, he wasn't *elected* until age forty-six. John F. Kennedy, however, holds the distinction for being the youngest president to *die* in office.

ROSS, Betsy

Waxing patriotic, we come to our venerated American flag, which we all know was designed and sewn by the deft hands of Betsy Ross. Unfortunately, this long-standing notion is a star-spangled myth and belongs in the hokum catalog under the letters B.R. The whole story came from the imaginative (or devious) mind of her grandson. No one knows the exact and precise evolvement of our present-day Old Glory, but its genesis is mostly traceable to the British Union flag, which also includes the colors red, white, and blue.

RUBBER TREES

Rubber is one of the most common multi-use products found in our modern world, yet few people know much about its source and production. Most believe it comes from only one type of tree, the *Hevea brasiliensis*. But rubber juice can come from numerous kinds of trees, even from plants. Snap off the stem of a dandelion or even a head of lettuce, and a sour milky substance will ooze out. This is latex—the basic material of raw rubber. It wouldn't be cost-effective to attempt producing rubber from earth's green overcoat, but in theory it is feasible. The whole world's potentially "abounce" with rubber!

RUMBLING STOMACHS
It happens to all people—rich or poor, fat or lean, gauche or dignified—the gurgles, burbles, swashing, and sloshing that are part of the gastronomical racket within the digestive recesses of the stomach. But all that racket doesn't really emanate from the tummy, as is generally supposed. That's because food *isn't* digested in the stomach, but in the *small* and *large intestines,* where air and liquefied food (chyme) move along their course in the digestive process. Solution? Grin and bear it; you are just experiencing "borborygmus"!

RUSSIA
Because of the revolutionary political events that took place in the former Soviet Union during the late 1980s and early 1990s, many people have become more knowledgeable about that particular geographic area. Yet the misconception lingers in the minds of most Americans that *Russia* and the *Soviet Union* were synonymous terms. They were not! Russia was but one of the fifteen republics of the former Union of Soviet Socialist Republics.

S

SACCHARIN
Artificial sweeteners have entered the food chain only recently, with improvements being made each year. An example is saccharin. Many people assume that saccharin is a recent development, which it isn't. What were U.S. chemists Ira Remsen and Constantine Fahlberg looking for back in

1879 while investigating coal tar derivatives? They were interested in tar acids, phenolic compounds that react with caustic soda and other chemicals. But of all things they least expected to find among those laboratory bitters was a substance that would have 500 times the sweetening power of table sugar. They were trying to determine its suitability for human consumption well over one hundred years ago.

SAE NUMBER

The letters *SAE* are familiar to most automobile drivers even though many don't have a clue as to their meaning—"slick and easy"? "stop an engine"? Anyway, the acronym is a code established by the U.S. Society of Automobile Engineers to specify the viscosity of lubricating oil, a term that determines how readily oil flows—how thin or thick it is. But what about the *W* that accompanies the SAE code? Many drivers believe it stands for "weight." It doesn't! Rather, it stands for "winter," indicating that the oil is suitable for colder weather. All motor oils weigh virtually the same regardless of the code. When service station attendants ask drivers (who don't know viscosity from peanut butter) what type of oil they prefer, they usually receive an answer like: "Well now, sir, what kind of oil would *you* suggest that I use this particular month!" Everybody is happy!

SAFETY GLASS

(another one of those surprisingly early innovations). When the windshield glass on those old Model-T Ford automobiles was hit by flying rocks, it was a shattering experience for the driver—glass on the seat and the street and in milady's hair, everywhere! Those early windshields were accidents just waiting to happen, and many people were injured by them. It wasn't long before automobile manufacturers began assembling the newer models with shatterproof safety glass, a glass that still hasn't been perfected. But few people today realize how long ago the first safety glass was introduced—not in

Henry Ford's day, but considerably earlier. Frenchman Edouard Benedictus, artist and chemist, was probably considered to be a few bubbles short when he laminated a piece of celluloid between two pieces of glass back in 1909, but the lamination proved to be so effective that he was issued a patent on the crazy idea that eventually led to what we have today.

SAGEBRUSH

The bushy aromatic plant that served as the frontier cowboy's bed and which gives floral character to the western and prairie states is not at all related to the true sage used for food seasoning. Rather it is a shrub of the genus *Artemisia* that received its name from the sweet, sagelike odor of its crushed foliage. If you have a recipe that calls for sage you'd better shake the spice out of a can, because a meal seasoned with sagebrush would surely foul up the bacon and beans.

SAHARA DESERT

The vast forbidding land mass occupying almost all of the northern part of the African continent is often mistakenly regarded as a totally flat, waterless wasteland, supersaturated with shifting sand and void of living matter. From a topographical standpoint, we have to scotch that notion because there is much variation in Sahara's landscape. The great desert has 600- to 1,200-foot plains, 400-foot lowlands and depressions, and two mountain chains, the highest rising to a height of 11,204 feet—the Tibesti mountains. Inhospitable as the Sahara is, only about 20 percent of it is sand, and in some areas there are even underground streams. On occasion, upon deep diggings into the sand to reach fresh water, live fish have been detected. A minor point: When we refer to this land as the Sahara Desert we are being redundant. The word *Sahara* means "desert," and using the term as such is like saying *desert desert*.

ST. AUGUSTINE, FLORIDA

Most textbooks and encyclopedias identify St. Augustine, Florida, as the oldest city in the United States. But that depends! It didn't begin as a city, only a settlement. When Spaniard Pedro Menéndez de Aviles booted the French out of their hastily built Fort Caroline establishment in 1565, St. Augustine was founded, slowly developing into a modern city. But up in the sunny mesa in the New Mexico desert, you can see another settlement, one that began about 500 years before the predatory Pedro was born. The Pueblo Indian village of Acoma, New Mexico, has been an active, flourishing community for 1,000 years, having withstood myriad tribal assaults and conflicts and the brutal pillaging by the Spanish occupation. St. Augustine the oldest community in the United States? Not by a half millennium!

SALES TAX

The term *sales tax* is both a misconception and a misnomer. It isn't the *seller* (the supermarket) that pays the tax on your groceries, it is *you,* the consumer. It is therefore more correctly a *purchase* tax or a consumer tax rather than a sales tax. An *excise tax* comes closer to the mark as it defines a tax levied by the government on the manufacturer and/or on the seller of the goods. But that doesn't make much sense either, because the tax invariably trickles down to the buyer, making him the taxpayer after all. A severance tax, where companies are taxed on minerals, oil, or timber severed from the earth, also inevitably is a tax that is ultimately taken from the pockets of John Q. Public.

SALT

What comes to mind when people think of salt? food seasoning, the white grainy stuff we shake into our soup and onto our beef and spuds. Contrary to common understanding, however, the use of salt for seasoning food is by far one of the lesser uses we have for the important mineral. There are 14,000 different uses mankind has for salt. In addition to its myriad uses in food processing, salt is utilized in meat packing, chemical manufacturing, hide and leather processing, and the production of soda ash (a substance used in making soap, glass, and washing compounds). It is also used in the electrolysis process, to whiten paper and to purify water. In fact, less than 4 percent of all salt produced each year in North America finds its way to family dining tables, either in commercially processed foods, in home preparations, or in the salt shaker. Another mistaken idea is that most salt is mined in the west. Actually, New York State produces more salt than any other state. Few people understand the historic significance of salt. It served as money at various times and places, and has been the cause of bitter warfare. A far-flung trade in ancient Greece involving the exchange of salt for slaves gave rise to the expression "not worth his salt." Special salt rations given to early Roman soldiers were know as *salarium argentum,* the forerunner of the English word *salary.* There are more than thirty references to salt in the Bible. Visit a salt mine and descend to the 2,000-foot level; it's a strange white world down there!

SALT CONTRIBUTES TO HIGH BLOOD PRESSURE

Health-conscious people have been railing against salt for so many years it's doubtful the brackish stuff will ever be cleared of contempt. But the briny compound has weathered worse insults than the claim that it causes hypertension, heart disease, and uric-acid gout, and that it aggravates the problems relating to ill-fitting shoes. It now appears those pejorative slaps at salt are rapidly beginning to be discredited. The more recent and more objective international studies now show that weight and age, and a gaggle of other factors, are far more reliable predictors of high blood pressure than is salt intake. If the *British Medical Journal* (February, 1988) can be called reliable, then we must conclude that salt, the supposed hypertension villain, is rather a benign culprit that still hasn't been topped as a necessary food seasoning. Besides, asks the *Journal,* how do we explain the fact that the salt-loving Japanese have a significantly lower level of high blood pressure than do the sodium abstainers of most other countries? Looks like salt still hasn't lost its savor!

SAMSON AND DELILAH
Contrary to general opinion, the betrayal of Samson by the cunning Delilah was not Samson's first and only experience in tragic romancing and uncontrolled rampaging. Notwithstanding Samson's birth being foretold by angels, his physical endowment of extraordinary strength undoubtedly also led to his being a womanizer. As he matured, he would often visit the Philistines in their coastal cities wherein he engaged in a bit of Old Testament girl watching. On one occasion he demanded his father procure for him a Philistine woman who had attracted him. She later betrayed him as a result of his revealing the legendary "riddle of the lion and swarm of bees." After the commotion he caused in another Judaean town where he was bound by the townspeople and put on trial, Samson went to the city of Gaza where again he gave in to his passions by sleeping with a harlot. While he was asleep she told his enemies of his whereabouts, resulting in his being again bound and readied to be killed. (It wasn't Delilah who actually cut his hair.) Having learned firsthand about Philistine go-go girls, the Hebrew hulk should have been more suspicious of the beguiling Delilah, but "street smart" he was not!

SANDERS, Colonel (Kentucky Fried Chicken)
Madison Avenue would be hard-pressed to create a more colorful figure than Harland Sanders, the chicken-frying Kentucky colonel who, at age sixty, started up the largest cackle franchise in the world. But notwithstanding the clever portrayal, Sanders was not a commissioned officer with the

rank of colonel; his title was an *honorary* one granted him in 1936 by the governor of Kentucky. The only actual military experience he had was one year spent in Cuba as a soldier in the United States Army. (Such honorary titles, particularly that of colonel, have been bestowed on numerous men in the past for various reasons, and have even been the stereotype trademark for whisky, coal, and tobacco during the early part of this century.) Another misconception about the finger-lickin' entrepreneur has to do with his birthplace, which wasn't Kentucky but Henryville, Indiana, the state where he spent most of his youth working at sundry low-paying jobs.

SANTA CLAUS
This information probably won't disturb the millions of tots who sit on Santa Claus's lap each December, but their parents may want to tell them (without revealing that St. Nick is a non-person) that this ho-ho fellow's first name—Santa—is not really a first name at all. The word *Santa* is his *title*, which comes from the Dutch term Sinter-Klaas—the name of the boy-bishop and patron saint of Myra, Turkey, whose actual name was St. Nicholas. To most adults, the notion that such an altruistic person actually lived and delivered presents to children and the needy is pure myth, but the story is actually based on truth. Young Nicholas was a kind and caring little Turk who, around 300 A.D., went out at night taking gifts to the many needy persons of his impoverished hamlet. As to Santa's *last* name, he doesn't really have one.

SAUNAS AND BODY TOXINS
Do saunas really cleanse the body of toxins, as many health peddlers believe? Well, they make you perspire a lot, but beyond that, the notion they somehow detoxify the torso is false. The unbearable sauna heat does enhance blood flow near the surface of the skin, but the sweating doesn't rid the body of bacteria any more than would a warm shower. The

Finns are noted for their unmerciful tree-branch flailing of each other's nakedness while in a sauna, which supposedly increases blood circulation, but circulation is not excretion. The body-cleansing notion may date back to Herodotus, who, in 500 B.C., wrote of the inhabitants of Scythia, Central Eurasia, throwing water and hemp seed on heated stones to create an intoxicating steam. But, again, intoxication is not detoxification.

SCHIZOPHRENIA

The fact that this rather inscrutable word actually means "split mind" (from Greek *schizo*—to split, and Greek *phren*—mind) makes it quite natural that early psychologists would refer to schizophrenia as the split-personality disorder. However, such is not the case. A person with this particular disorder doesn't have more than one personality; that's an entirely different syndrome. Although there are many subvarieties of schizophrenia (the most consistent characteristics being an apathy or indifference to reality and social relationships, and a dissociation of thoughts and ideas from normal emotions), none relate to multiple personalities. The irony is that given the strangeness of the sickness, a person with schizophrenia might be the first to admit to *having* a split personality.

SEA LEVEL

Sea level is often erroneously regarded as a fixed starting point for measuring height or depth—a position where air interfaces with water. It would surprise most people to learn that the level of the sea is not exactly the same in all parts of the world, but changes constantly at every locality with the tides, atmospheric pressure, wind conditions, and the earth's changing climates. People cooking hot dogs on the beach during low tide would have their weenies soaked if they stayed at the same spot during high tide. In other words, when it's low tide somewhere on the ocean shoreline, it is high tide somewhere else. As a measuring medium, sea level is only an agreed-upon average, or *mean level,* that scientists use to make their calculations.

SEVEN SEAS/SEVEN OCEANS

The vast amount of water that covers nearly three-quarters of the earth's surface is divided into what we traditionally call the seven seas, or seven oceans, namely, the South and North Pacific, the South and North Atlantic, the Indian, the Arctic, and the Antarctic. But these oceans are not really separate bodies of water as are the giant inland lakes bordered by land. They exist only by artificial definition. A brief survey of a global map will show there is, in reality, only *one* ocean— plenty of open water for a nonstop canoe trip.

SHAKESPEARE, William

The Horatio Alger rags-to-riches theme has even included the likes of the incomparable playwright William Shake-speare, who has often been characterized as a poor, virtually uneducated village bumpkin who fled from Stratford to London to escape prosecution for poaching on the lands of Sir Thomas Lucy. In truth, his father was a respected, relatively wealthy man who held several municipal offices and who married into an equally distinguished Catholic family, where it was assured that young William would be given an intensive grammar school education, which included Latin and Greek. Also, most people want to keep Shakespeare tightly wrapped in his prissy pantaloons as if he had no other interests except the theater. Actually, in addition to marrying and fathering children, he engaged in many temporal, nonthespian activities, including the acquisition of substantial holdings of real estate, particularly around Stratford.

SHALE OIL

The term *shale oil* is a misnomer; it is neither shale nor oil.
Simply put, the rock is limestone, and the "oil" it contains is a
waxy hydrocarbon substance called kerogen, a sludgy goo
that, unlike conventional crude oil, requires the removal of
many chemicals during the refining process. The extraction
of "oil" from "shale" on a grand scale for industrial use may
be a twentieth-century idea, but the *use* of shale oil ("the rock
that burns") for more utilitarian purposes dates back to very
early times. Centuries before, resourceful Scottish farmers
were known to obtain oil by firing up batches of rocks that
contained the "oyle" they needed for cooking. In 1694, a
patent was recorded in London for extracting "oyle" from
rock.

SHAMU, the Killer Whale

Virtually everyone has enjoyed the Sea World show featuring
the antics of the lovable whale named Shamu, whose favorite
whalish trick is swimming close to the pool's edge and giving
the first five rows of people an unceremonious baptism. But
the name Shamu is not the name given to just *one* killer whale
but several. It is a trademark name for all the whales who
perform in four different Sea World entertainment parks in
San Diego, San Antonio, Cleveland, and Orlando. The name
Shamu has no particular significance other than the fact that
Sea World wanted a name similar to that of its first whale,
whose name was Namu. (*See also* Killer Whales.)

SHERIFF

No symbol has become more a part of the national character
of America than that of the sheriff. But this county law-
enforcing constable is by no means indigenous to the United
States. Sheriffs were in place in England long before America was discovered—back as far as the Norman Conquest in
1066. The word *sheriff* comes from two sources: *shire* and
reeve. In Old England, each shire (county) had a headman

known as a reeve. The singular word *sheriff* is thus a combination of those two words. Law-enforcement officers are also referred to as sheriffs in Canada, Scotland, and Northern Ireland.

SHOOTING STARS
So-called shooting stars are not distant, giant stars or stellar bodies hurtling through the universe, rather they are tiny sand-sized pieces of metallic or stony matter that enter our atmosphere at speeds great enough to cause them to burn up before striking the ground. Known as meteoroids, they become visible at about sixty-five miles above the earth's surface, heat up by air friction to about 4,000°F, and blink out in the twinkle of an eye.

SIAMESE TWINS
On rare occasions some twins are born joined together at some point of their anatomy, the most notable example being the famous Siamese Twins of Bangkok. The infants were attached together at the breastbone. Since their birth in May 1911, all such twins have been referred to as Siamese twins (even by some in the medical field). This is a mistake! The correct term for this twinship condition is not *Siamese* twins but *conjoined* twins. In 1980, two infants joined together at the head were separated in a delicate, first-time operation at the University of Utah Medical Center in Salt Lake City. Doctors properly referred to the children as *conjoined* twins. As a point of interest, the original and much celebrated Siamese twins didn't live a life of total helplessness and despair as most people have imagined, but took advantage of their anomalous condition by making public appearances; they eventually became wealthy landowners, married, sired twenty-two children, and later retired (The part about siring twenty-two children is most intriguing.)

SIERRA NEVADA MOUNTAIN RANGE

Despite its name, which suggests that this 400-mile granite mountain range is located in the state of Nevada, it is actually situated between the Great Basin and the Central Valley of *California.* Three of our country's most visited attractions and national parks are within its 31,000-square mile boundaries—Lake Tahoe, Yosemite, and Sequoia National Parks. None of the Sierra Nevada is in Nevada, but no Nevadan is willing to give up the name!

SITTING BULL

This legendary hero, born and raised in what is now South Dakota, was originally given the name Jumping Badger, but because as a boy he showed great bravery in a fight against the Crow Indians, his name was changed to Sitting Bull, an honor bestowed on him by his father, whose name was also Sitting Bull. Well, as brave as the old brave was, his story happens to be sitting on a pile of bull! It wasn't *he* who led the attack against General George Custer at the Battle of the Little Big Horn in 1876, but another warrior leader named Crazy Horse. Sitting Bull was the tribe's leading *medicine man,* who actually did more sitting than fighting during that famous battle. The real flash point that precipitated the fierce fighting to come, however, *was* a result of Sitting Bull's prophesying that they must change their way of fighting and adopt a fight-to-kill attitude or they would lose all their lands to the whites. (His prophecy was made during a sun dance.) Anyway, Sitting Bull and other practitioners of his day apparently pulled a lot of weight among the Indian people, even if their healing skills didn't win many wars.

SKIN

Much to the surprise of many, the heaviest organ of the human body is not the heart, liver, or lungs; it is the *skin.* Weighing in at about eighteen pounds for the average adult, and measuring approximately eighteen square feet, this complex organic garment has at least four major functions: maintaining body temperature and fluid balance, shielding the body from foreign forms intent on invasion, synthesizing essential hormones and other biochemicals, and serving as the first receptive sensor for interpreting the tactile messages given by others. It is indeed an organ in the truest sense, and like all other body organs must be protected for optimal functioning. Another misconception about the skin is that it is only a covering, under which all the blood supply is maintained. Wrong! Our skin is not only protectional, it is also functional. Healthy skin contains and uses about one-fourth of the body's total blood supply in order to carry out its important cover-up job.

SLEEP
Ah, sleep! Sweet, sweet sleep—a time for the body to rest! But is it? It's bedtime and your body and brain have performed their slave labor for the day. It is now time to recharge the system. Logic tells us that's the only purpose of sleep. But science says no, because while the body is unconscious, a lot of busy body maintenance is taking place. During sleep the body steps up its production of protein and growth hormones. Sleep is patch-up time, when repairs are made and dead cells replaced. And when we are sleeping, we dream. Some persons swear they don't, but the fact of the matter is, all humans dream; remembering the crazy drama is another question. (See the entry entitled Dreams.)

SLEEPING ON THE LEFT SIDE
The taboo against sleeping on the left side of the body has been around probably since the days when everyone thought the heart was located on the body's left side. (We still cover the left side of our chest when we repeat the Pledge of Allegiance, do we not?) Today, however, we are supposedly more knowledgeable, yet this throw-back idea still persists. One may start out sleeping on the right side, but, according

to the legitimate research done on sleep patterns, the left side of the body will get its share of sack time regardless. And the heart won't know the difference!

SMALL CLAIMS COURT

Those who think winning a money judgment in a small claims court is tantamount to *collecting* the money may be in for a surprise. The court is not obligated to *enforce* a judgment and collect your money; you have to do it yourself. And if the debtor hasn't got enough money for a fast-food cheeseburger, collecting on a judgment may have to be deferred until the millennium. It also means that levying on wages, bank accounts, business assets, or real property won't do the trick either if there is nothing on which to levy. An experience in a small claims court can be an eye-opener!

SMALLPOX VACCINATIONS

The notion persists that persons traveling to certain foreign countries still must receive smallpox vaccinations in order to obtain a visa for such travel. Because it has been many years since the disease has been seen in any country, smallpox vaccinations are no longer a prerequisite for obtaining a visa.

SNAFU

The clever acronym SNAFU, which stands for Situation Normal: All Fouled Up, was not an original with American GIs. Though used extensively by our troops during World War II, they borrowed it from the British blokes with whom the GIs often fraternized.

SOS

The emergency call sign SOS is not really a true acronym as is generally supposed. Many meanings of this international distress symbol have been conjured up in the past, such as "Save our Ship," etc., but the fact is that of all the alphabet letters, *S* and *O* are the simplest and easiest to visually identify and to transmit physically. Try tapping out any other combinations of letters of the alphabet and you'll find that simplicity in sending and receiving is the only logical reason for the selection. (Just in case you get shanghaied to some lonely island and are fortunate enough to be provided with telegraphic equipment, you may wish to know the letters would be tapped out as follows: ···————···.)

SOUND

Despite the fact that most people think sound travels at an absolute fixed speed, they stand to be corrected. There is no such thing as a constant speed of sound. It varies according to the density and elasticity of the medium through which it travels (16,000 feet a second through steel, 11,900 feet a second through brick, 4,700 feet a second through water, and 1,100 feet a second through air). Even temperature affects the speed of sound. In a vacuum where there is no density and no elasticity, we can expect sound not to travel at all, and it doesn't.

SPANISH CONQUISTADORS

History continues to be unkind to those spindly legged, rooster-helmeted, sixteenth-century conquistadors of Mexico and Peru, and rightfully so. They ruthlessly plundered and brutalized the native people of those lands. But in spite of the bad-actor Spaniards who were in it only for gold and riches, not all conquistadors had such evil intentions. Some were scholars who chronicled the events of that period with honest intent, exercising benevolence and befriending the natives so that authentic histories could be preserved.

SPEED AND VELOCITY

Contrary to what is commonly thought, speed and velocity are not the same thing. To make a long paragraph short, speed indicates the rate of motion in any direction. Velocity, on the other hand, indicates the rate of motion in one *fixed* direction. In other words, velocity is a mathematical vector quantity that designates not only how fast, but in what direction, a body is moving. It has both speed and direction. (And that, no doubt, is as clear as Mississippi mud.)

SPIDERS
Despite the vehement objections spiders have to being called insects, it's a losing battle for the abhorrent arthropods; people will always believe they are indeed insects! But *spiders* know who they are as well as their cousins, the daddy longlegs and mites, and the more distantly related scorpions and crabs. Spiders identify with that snobby class called arachnids, and the only insecty thing about them is their diet, which consists of real insects. For people afflicted with arachnophobia, this information probably won't help at all, but bear in mind: spiders do a lot of beneficial trench work, keeping other beastly little crawling things from inheriting the earth.

SPINACH
There's no question that Popeye has been as great a salesman for spinach as Lee Iacocca has been for the Chrysler Corporation. The only difference is that there is more credibility in Iacocca's car claims than there is in spinach's energy claims. Spinach simply isn't a high-energy food, nor is it especially noted for its iron content—about 3 parts of iron for 100,000 parts of spinach, most of which the body doesn't absorb anyway. Although Popeye's delight and other leafy veggies are rich in some other minerals and vitamins, there is no truth to the assumption that they build strong bodies. Besides, Popeye eats spinach right out of the can, where it's already lost much of the ergonomic value it started with.

SPOONS AND CUPS
Having given little or no thought to the dimensions and capacities of some of our most common kitchen items, we

tend to think spoons and cups measure exactly alike. This is not always true! The probability is that products of the *same manufacturer* will measure the same but not necessarily those of *different* manufacturers. "Close enough" seems to be an acceptable standard with the spoon and cup makers of America. Speaking of spoons, one doesn't have to be a teaspoon short to believe that two teaspoons equal a tablespoon, because many people are of that opinion. But good measuring tells us that it takes *three* teaspoons to make a tablespoon, not two. So if the family only gives Mom a C-minus for her spice cake, she may want to check out her spoonology.

SPOT REDUCING

Don't fall for it! It doesn't work! In the business of weight reduction there's no magic bullet that will hit an exclusive "problem area" and leave everything else intact. That's because weight loss is *proportional.* In toning a particular part of the body such as the stomach (by sit-ups, for instance), all the weight loss doesn't come only from fat stored around the tummy, but from the fat stored throughout the entire body. Therefore, any weight loss realized from the exercise would be a dividend to the body as a whole, not just the stomach, albeit muscle toning for the stomach can indeed strengthen and tone the abdominal muscles, resulting in better support for the back. In the final analysis, bulge reduction is simply a matter of *burning* excess calories. So it looks as if that vibrating belt used in health spas won't do any more for girth reduction than the belt used to hold up your trousers!

SPRUCE GOOSE

When the unpredictable entrepreneur Howard Hughes built his eight-engine, 329-foot-wingspan flying boat in the early 1940s, he couldn't use war-shortage metal, so he opted for wood. Unfortunately, the plane (designed to carry troops and cargo for 3,000 miles) turned out to be a disaster! Not only was the big bird, which flew a total of only one mile, badly designed, mismanaged, and cost-overrridden, it was further disgraced by being called by the wrong name—*Spruce Goose*. Although Hughes knew the beast was actually made of *birch*—and personally despised the derisive term—the popularity of its rhyming name eventually won the day.

STALIN, Joseph
The infamous Joseph Stalin was indeed generalissimo and premier of the Soviet Union, but he was not Russian as is most generally supposed, nor was his real name Joseph Stalin. The ruthless Bolshevik with the gunslinger mustache was born Iosif Vissarionivich Dzhugashvili in Georgia, a southern province of the former Soviet Union.

STANDISH, Miles
Here we go again—another case of Longfellow's carelessness with the facts. A good poet but a not-so-good researcher, Longfellow gets unduly imaginative when he infers, in his poem "The Courtship of Miles Standish," that John Alden was asked by Standish to propose marriage for him to Priscilla Mullins. There is no historical evidence whatsoever to support that aspect of the poem.

STONEHENGE
Riding, by tourist bus, about eight miles north from Salisbury, Wiltshire, England, you will come to an odd, circular arrangement of stones surrounded by an earthwork. The place is called Stonehenge, and if the tour guide is knowledgeable he will advise you that although most people think the curiosity was built by the Druids, they would nevertheless be wrong. The supposed connection with the Druids has no basis at all inasmuch as Stonehenge was built during the Bronze Age. The Druids identify with the later Iron Age. Also, notwithstanding the many theories as to Stonehenge's actual purpose (including the latest claim that it was some

kind of astronomical calendar), the jury is still out on its real purpose.

STOP SIGNS
As much as this may sound like an attempt to beat the system, not all stop signs have to be obeyed. Many shopping malls, health spas, condominium developments, and other privately owned properties have stop signs on their premises but, in many instances, heeding them is actually not enforceable. There are a variety of rules and regulations within each state regarding such signs, but one thing is usually standard: If a privately owned commercial facility has made arrangements with its municipality to have the streets on its property *dedicated,* then its stop signs must be honored like those on public roads and thoroughfares. But many places haven't taken the time to make such arrangements; thus stopping at their stop signs is not legally enforceable.

STRADIVARI VIOLINS
The legendary Stradivari violins made by Italian violin maker Antonio Stradivari have long been held up as the quintessential model of instrument craftsmanship. Upon his death in 1737, the little fiddle maker had made more violins than his instrumental mind could recall. But contrary to common knowledge, Stradivari made far more *other* instruments than violins. He also made equally fine cellos and violas, not to mention lutes, viols, guitars, mandolins, and bows. But it wasn't only the craftsmanship itself that gave his violins their unmatched sound, it was the varnish the old master used to treat his wood—a secret just recently discovered. In 1984, the Landolfi String Quartet of St. Louis played a concert using violins treated with the newly discovered gook; both critics and players agreed they had achieved that unmistakable Stradivari sound.

STRESS

All stress is bad for you! That's what they say. Of course, the concept of stress is an abstraction, and no one knows more about that stressful abstraction than Hans Selye, the Canadian doctor/scientist. Selye points to both good and bad types of stress. The unpleasant, disease-producing kind is called distress; the pleasant or curative kind is called eustress—that which Selye refers to as "stress without distress." Says Selye, "Stress is not necessarily bad for you; it is the spice of life, for any emotion, any activity causes stress. But, of course, your system must be prepared to take it."

STRESS IN THE WORKPLACE

A lot has been written about "stress in the workplace," but most of it is incorrect. The most current findings tell us people sometimes do become unglued in their particular type of work, but not necessarily in the high-pressure jobs. The new studies show conclusively that the so-called high-pressure jobs (even for the so-called type-A personalities) are not necessarily the high-stress jobs. Rather it is the *boring,* clock-watching jobs, with rigid procedures, restricted creative opportunities, and limitations in decision-making, that produce the greatest personal stress in the workplace—the jobs of telephone operators, nurses, assembly-line workers, waitresses, and other jobs where the work environment places a strain on a person's equilibrium. High-performance jobs—those of executives, surgeons, engineers, money managers, and other professionals—may be demanding as to hours and workload, but they are considered low-stress jobs when there are opportunities for advancement, freedom in decision-making, and chances to take initiative. In other words, the low-stress jobs are the high-ladder jobs if the work is enjoyed.

SUBLIMINAL MESSAGES

Subliminal advertising is not a contemporary thing, having been used in one form or another for over seventy years. But thanks to the now-famous marketing experiment imposed on the unsuspecting patrons of a Fort Lee, New Jersey, movie theater in 1957 (supposedly causing a frenzy of Coke- and popcorn-buying during intermission), the notion that people can be subconsciously compelled to buy things through such split-second imagery has become an accepted belief. Not so! Subliminal perception has few serious advocates within the scientific community. One subliminal debunker, Canadian psychologist Dr. Timothy Moore, along with a sizable quorum of other skeptics, asserts that the sneaky messages are typically benign and ineffectual, and have no apparent relevance to the goals of advertising. Moore further states that although the messages are a clever marketing scheme, they have not accomplished their intended job of commercial brainwashing. Incidentally, the Fort Lee foray was at best amateurish—not reported and not supported by a single reputable scientific journal, and never replicated.

SUBMARINES

The stealthy submarine first became a major factor in naval warfare during World War I when Germany employed them as commerce destroyers. That fact, along with the resounding success of their U-boat assaults against enemy ships during World War II, has led many to believe that the Germans invented the submarine. They didn't, although they wish they did. So did individuals like Herodotus, Aristotle, Leonardo da Vinci, and Pliny the Elder, all of whom mentioned attempts to build submarinelike contraptions for various purposes. The credit for building the first submarine probably goes to Holland's Cornelius Van Drebel in about the year 1600, when he maneuvered his graceless contrivance a few meters beneath the surface during repeated trials in the Thames River in England. But the Dutchman's oddity qualified more for spooking the carp than it did for practical utility, and was soon abandoned. The first *useful* submarine built as an offensive naval weapon, however, was the *Turtle*, a one-man craft invented by David Bushnell, a student at Yale. Bushnell's craft was built during the American Revolution, with the purpose of approaching the British warship H.M.S. *Eagle,* and sinking it. From that time on, American ingenuity for building submarines became clearly evident, with the United States making most of the important innovative developments up to the present time. At any rate, many nations had a go at serious sub building before Germany did.

SUGAR, SWEET SUGAR

For at least two decades sugar has been villainized as a junk-food indulgence that supposedly causes heart disease, obesity, cavities, hyperactivity, diabetes, hangnails, flat feet, B.O., ad infinitum. Here are some of the dulcet misconceptions, written as true/false questions:

a. Sugarless gum contains fewer calories than sugared gum. False! This sweet-as-ever gum without the sucrose is supposed to help us with our cavity problems, all without calories, the happy ads imply. But we shouldn't kid ourselves into thinking we're ingesting fewer calories, because sugarless gum contains a substance called sorbitol, a type of sugar that has as many calories as table sugar.

b. Eating too much sugar causes diabetes. False! This misconception arises because diabetes is characterized by high levels of blood sugar (glucose). Excessive sugar consumption is indeed very dangerous for diabetics who must curtail their sugar intake, but sugar doesn't *cause* the disorder.

c. Artificial sweeteners will make you lose weight. False! Studies have failed to show that artificial sweeteners help people lose anything—especially weight. Artificial sweeteners don't suppress appetite; moreover, they keep the sweet tooth in a begging mode as does real sugar.

d. Sugar is the leading cause of obesity. False! Two studies in 1988 by the *American Journal of Nutrition* found that for most people, the majority share of excess calories (leading to obesity) comes from eating too much fat, not sugar. The *Journal* concluded that lean people tend to eat more sugar and less fat that obese persons. We often blame sugary foods for weight gain, forgetting that the cakes, ice cream, chocolate, and cookies we're eating derive most of their calories from fat, not sugar. And many people admitting to having a sweet tooth may in fact have a "fat tooth." So, primarily, it is calories, not sugar, that causes greater weight gain.

e. A person can become addicted to sugar. False! There's no evidence to support the assertion that people can be physically addicted to sugar, with the physical withdrawal symptoms associated with truly addictive substances. Other foods such as bananas of dried fruit may raise blood sugar just as much as table sugar, but no one claims they're addictive.

f. Sugar in fruit is good, sugar in candy is bad. False! The sugar in most fruit is primarily fructose, which has few if any advantages over sucrose. Like other sugars, it is converted to glucose in the body. Fruit actually contains a combination of fructose, sucrose, and glucose. The one good thing about getting your sugar from fruit rather than from candy and colas is that it comes with vitamins, minerals, and fiber, while the sugary snacks provide only empty calories.

g. A product labeled "sugarless" contains no sugar forms. False! This sin-of-omission label means only that the product contains no sucrose—or table sugar. A further check will probably show that it includes other kinds of sugar—fructose, sorbitol, or glucose. Artificial sweeteners, however, meet the *sugarless* criteria.

SUICIDES DURING HOLIDAYS

Concomitant with the coming of the Christmas season, as well as other major holiday periods, we can expect that other predictable portent—the idea that the nation's suicide rate will rise to the holiday occasion. In light of the latest statistical studies on the holiday/suicide syndrome, such a connection has to be summarily discarded. At least that's what the charts at the National Center for Health Statistics are showing. The folks at the center aren't joking when they point to April as the month when most self-destruction takes place, not December, as most of us have been led to believe. Notwithstanding the fact that spring is nature's rebirth period, it is also, inexplicably, the peak period for many people who seem compelled to end it all. The holidays turn out to be the days when the *fewest* suicides take place.

SUN'S DISTANCE FROM EARTH

One of the most universally held misconceptions we earthlings have about our universe relates to the closeness of the sun to our own planet Earth. Conventional wisdom dictates that the sun is farthest from the earth during the wintertime, which is the reason the old homestead becomes so shivery cold during that period. But there's a misconception here! Because the earth's orbit is elliptic, its distance from the sun varies during the year, making it actually closest to the sun on January 3, when it is 91,410,000 miles away. On July 4, when you can fry a duck egg on the sidewalk, the earth is at its *greatest* distance from the sun—94,519,000 miles—give or take an arm's length or two.

SUN'S TEMPERATURE

Contrary to popular opinion, the sun's surface temperature is not all that hot. (Relatively speaking, that is.) What *is* hot is the corona that surrounds it—hotter by a blistering degree. Never mind what the second law of thermodynamics has to say about heat not transferring from a cooler to a hotter body, the fact is the sun's surface is relatively cool (6,000°C compared to the 3,000,000°C for the corona). Of course, the fastest suntan can be gotten from deep within the sun, where El Sol gets up to 15,000,000°C. Another misconception about the sun: It doesn't emit a *steady* stream of light as most of us may think, it actually pulsates or flickers.

SUNTAN
The notion has somehow developed that suntans received in today's modern tanning salons are not harmful to the skin. This is a sunburned notion at best! The procedures for beaming ultraviolet light onto lily-white bodies in these vanity salons don't preclude dangerous light rays from doing their damage if proper precautions are not taken. The FDA requires sunlamp manufacturers to sell protective goggles along with their sunlamps, but the salons need not require customers to wear them. In short, tanning salons, despite claims to the contrary, are no safer today than before.

SURVIVAL OF THE FITTEST
We erroneously suppose the term "survival of the fittest" has to do only with survivability in a physically superlative sense—the strongest and the fiercest. This is not always true. For instance, a particular animal that is better able to *hide* from its enemies (and therefore live longer to produce more offspring) may prove to be more fit than a species inclined to get into toothy encounters with other animals, thereby cutting short its life. An example would be the saber-toothed tiger. Actually, any trait that lengthens an animal's life span, that improves its access to members of the opposite sex, or both, will enhance fitness and resultant survivability of that particular animal.

SWALLOWS RETURNING TO CAPISTRANO
The faithful, unerring return of the little swallows to San Juan Capistrano on the same date, St. Joseph's Day, March

19, is ridiculous nonsense to those who know better, and especially to the residents of Capistrano, who have seen the little aves cruise in, on many occasions, in late February and the end of March. Birds migrate according to their own instinctive calendar, not our nonintuitive Gregorian calendar.

SWASTIKA

The equilateral cross with arms bent at right angles—the swastika—is so generally ascribed to Nazi Germany that it has become the modern world's symbol of hate. But the emblem is by no means original to that movement. It dates back to ancient Mesopotamia and appears in early Christian and Byzantine art. It is also clearly evident in the New World as well, most notably in the Mayan culture of South America and among the Navahos of North America, signifying prosperity and good fortune. A distinction is made between the right-hand swastika, which moves clockwise, and the left-hand swastika (the sauvastika), which moves in a counterclockwise direction. The right-hand swastika (the one gracing the arm of der fitful Führer) is considered a solar symbol representing the sun moving from east to south and thence to the west.

SWIMMING AFTER EATING

The Red Cross, which probably started the whole notion that swimming immediately after eating a meal is deleterious to one's health (it published a water-safety pamphlet on the subject in 1940), did an about-face on the issue in 1989. It's amended publication now offers "no objection to people participating in aquatic activities immediately upon completing a meal." Likewise, the YMCA no longer adheres to the well-entrenched myth of swimmers going belly-up on full bellies. What's more, empty-stomach swimming isn't even apt to facilitate a good float.

SWISS LANGUAGE

People desiring to vacation in Switzerland, and who want to yodel off a few Swiss words to get by, should know that there is no single Swiss language; it is a multilingual country whose languages include German, French, Italian, and Romansh, a local dialect. Because of the language situation, the country has three official names—Schweiz in the German language, Suisse in the French language, and Svizzera in the Italian language. So if you like crazy quilts, you'll find the language situation in Switzerland much to your liking!

T

TARANTULA

Just when people were beginning to trust the big hairy tarantula spider for being a good guy and not a contemptuous poisoner, along comes the movie *Arachnophobia* with its weird illusions, and after a couple of hours of squirming with "Big Boy," they're ready to call in the SWAT team. Alas, crawling right out of the horror chambers of Hollywood, the myth of the poor tarantula lives on! We may choose to bash the hairy hulk for being ugly and creepy, but poisonous and menacing it is not. Beyond an occasional bite (when provoked) they are generally quite harmless. Some people even have them for pets. The folks in old Italy once believed the tarantula's bite caused a disease called *tarantism,* which supposedly compelled its victims to flail about and make uncontrollable noises. The cure was said to be a lively Italian folk dance that eventually came to be known as the *tarantella*.

TASTE

Today's foods offer a smorgasbord of choices, to the delight of the greediest gourmand. But the fact is, he will *taste* very little of them. That's because we don't differentiate between foods as much by *taste* as we do by *smell*. It is also why people with bad colds—those whose nasal passages have been completely shut off—find food to be quite tasteless. Our sense of taste responds to only four sensations—sweet, sour, salty and bitter, all of which have their own specific taste-bud areas. At the tip and front edges, the tongue is sensitive to sweet and salty tastes. The sides are more sensitive to sour, and the back of the tongue to bitter. All other food flavors are *smelled*. Also, contrary to what most of us think, the center of the tongue is not where the taste buds *are*, it is where they are *not*.

TELEVISION VIEWING

Who are America's biggest couch potatoes? Young people get off the hook on this one. According to researchers, TV in the typical American home is turned on 7 hours and 32 minutes a day, but most of the couch time isn't spent by the youngsters. The champion TV watchers turn out to be the *elderly*, especially women over age fifty-five, who log an average of 6 hours and 19 minutes per day. Men of that same age group use up 5 hours and 29 minutes of their otherwise busy day staring down the TV set. Kids are often accused of watching when they should be studying, but their viewing is only half that of their parents. Whatever reason twelve-to-seventeen-year-old girls have for less television viewing is debatable, but their TV addiction amounts to "only" 3 hours per day.

THANKSGIVING DAY
It is usually believed that the first Thanksgiving, where early colonists shared their pilgrim pie and roast turkey with their hungry, bewildered Indian friends, was the prototype of feast days that has continued each year, nonstop, since that historic 1621 feast at Plymouth, Massachusetts. But prior to the 1800s, a Thanksgiving day was only celebrated when an occasion arose that was deemed worthy of prompting a feast day—an occasion that evoked a true spirit of thankfulness. Moreover, that famous first feast wasn't a one-day deal either; it was actually a three-day harvest festival. And for the record, the idea for the fourth Thursday came as late as the Rooseveltian era in 1942.

THUMBS UP, THUMBS DOWN
According to popular belief, the thumbs-up, thumbs-down hand gesture was the Roman emperor's eminent method of bestowing grace or disgrace upon a defeated gladiator. This is not technically correct. In truth, the hand gestures were thumb *extended,* signifying disapproval, or thumb *closed,* signifying approval. There was no "up" or "down" about it. To be sure, the gladiators knew the signals!

TIDAL WAVES
Despite its name, a tidal wave has no connection with true tides. These phenomena, also called tsunamis or storm waves, are a result of hurricanes originating at great distances from the shore. True tides, on the other hand, are the rising and falling of ocean waters on a definite daily time schedule, and are caused by the pulling forces of the sun and the moon.

TIMBUKTU
The name Timbukto is often thought to be a fictitious place on the deserted end of nowhere, a place where adversaries would like to consign each other if they only knew where it

was. But if you were standing in West Africa's Mali, at 938 feet altitude, you'd be mingling with about 20,483 Timbuktuans in the actual town of Timbuktu (or Tombouctu). You would also be nine miles north of Kabara, its port, on the Niger River, on the southern boundary of the Sahara. Between March and June, the primary trading months, the population balloons to accommodate the market. Today, Timbuktu is a military and medical center and the administrative headquarters of the Republic of Mali.

TIN CANS

Who would ever think tin cans were not made of tin? Well, they're not! At least, most of the grocery-type cans are tinless. Because real tin is a high-cost metal, most so-called tin cans are made out of pressed steel, iron, or even aluminum. The only tin involved in a tin can is an outer coating only a fraction of a millimeter thick, the inside usually being coated with enamel to prevent discoloration of the contents. In 1795, the French Revolutionary Government announced a 12,000-franc prize to the person who could find an effective way of storing food. It canned the idea for about fourteen years until a Parisian candy-maker named Nicholas Appert pocketed the sum with an early version of the sealed can. How long can a non-tin tin can be expected to preserve food? Longer than you may think! In 1945 the Australian government's Commonwealth Scientific and Industrial Research Organization received a very old can of soup from its liaison officer in London, who verified, by chemical analysis, that the vegetable-beef contents were still edible and nutritious. The soup dated back to about the year 1853. Napoleon also used canned food to supply his Grand Army in its invasion of Russia.

TINFOIL

Another misconception about tin has to do with tinfoil. Most tinfoil is made from cheaper metals such as lead or aluminum. Some real tinfoil *is* actually manufactured, but it is rare, and certainly wouldn't be found in K-Mart.

TOKYO ROSE

Was there such a person as Tokyo Rose, the beguiling temptress with the sultry voice who broadcast propaganda to the Pacific battlefront troops of the South Pacific? Apparently not! Not according to the records of the U.S. government, despite its conviction of suspect Iva Toguri d'Aquino, a Japanese-American citizen who spent five years in the slammer for alleged treasonous acts against the country of her birth. Circumstances, naive mistakes, and a postwar climate for punishment, all conspired against the vilified but resolutely loyal Japanese-American typist who, in January of 1977, was finally and justifiably pardoned by outgoing President Gerald Ford. In the final analysis, Iva Toguri d'Aquino was *not* the mythical Tokyo Rose whom the government wanted so desperately to convict. Substantial evidence has never been found showing that such a person really existed.

TOOTHACHE

To the person who may be experiencing a toothache, an academic understanding of why a tooth hurts may be the last thing the sufferer wants to know. Nevertheless, just for the record, the cavity story must be told. It is generally assumed that the pain experienced from cavities (dental caries) actually comes from the cavity itself. But what really aches isn't the cavity; rather it is the *tissue* surrounding the cavity. The genesis of a cavity is the action of microorganisms upon ingested sugars and carbohydrates, which produces acids that eat away the tooth enamel, continuing on into the pulpy dentin. The unwelcome pain results from pressure impacting the tooth's exposed nerves. The best prevention? A toothbrush! Don't leave home without one!

TOUCH

Most of us humans tend to believe that "feeling" takes place in the topmost (outer layer) of the skin, but this is not so. It is in the second layer where the tactile messages are first picked up. The skin that actually touches objects has *no* feeling and eventually sloughs off and gets replaced over time. (Sort of like a snake, but a little more subtle!) Some of that outer skin contributes to the ring around the bathtub. It has been said there's a trick to every trade. Perhaps that's why safecrackers have been known to fine-tune their fingers with sandpaper, allowing for greater receptivity.

TOURIST ATTRACTIONS/NATIONAL PARKS

Probably no other national park is more widely known than Yellowstone National Park. It would therefore be only natural to assume that Yellowstone outdraws all other major parks in tourism. Such is not the case! Considerably more visitors toll up to the Great Smoky Mountains National Park in Tennessee, the state's number-one natural tourist attraction. As for man-made attractions, it's hard to believe that any such attraction would outdraw our national parks, but to find the ultimate sweepstakes winner for tourism, you have to go to the West Coast: it's the *San Francisco Golden Gate Bridge*. According to the United States Chamber of Commerce, the stately Golden Gate Bridge is king of the hill. Well over 125,000 vehicles cross the majestic bridge *daily*—many of them loaded with camera-carrying tourists.

TRITON, Neptune's Moon

With so many moon circling so many planets in our solar system, the experts can be forgiven for implying that all moons orbit their parent planets in the same direction. But our universe's renegade moon, Triton, boomerangs the planet Neptune in the *opposite* direction, giving rise to a quadrillion explanations as to why!

TWINKLING STARS

We see twinkling stars (suns), and we assume their twinkle emanates from the stars themselves. In truth, this is a blinking illusion. The unsteady pulsating we observe is a result only of the stars' light rays passing through moving layers of atmosphere that circle the earth. Our astronauts, in space above the atmosphere, see an incredible number of stars without a blinker in the lot—just steady points of light. This next bit of solar prattle may not baffle the astro buffs, but to most earthlings the size of stars is a much misunderstood question. Because our own sun is very large (about 865,000 miles in diameter), we tend to regard most suns as being equal to it. But stars come in all sizes. Consider this: Some stars, according to astronomers, have diameters of about 1 billion miles.

TWO BITS, FOUR BITS, SIX BITS

What is this bit about *bits* in our United States coinage? Many believe the term *bits* is just part of the argot of the crazy coin world, but such terms are not without rational foundation. Actually they do have something to do with the physical bit (structure) of early coins. For instance, the Spanish pillar dollar (piece of eight) that circulated in the new nation was actually cut into *eight* equal bits, like a ready-to-serve apple pie. A single cut-out piece of the coin pie was known as a one-bit piece, a larger section being two bits, etc. So now, with that U.S. quarter in your hand, you have what amounts to two of eight bits of an uncut dollar. A half dollar would turn out to be a ⁴/₈ bit piece. So, how many bits do we need today for a shave and a haircut?

TWO-BY-FOURS

The standard wood timbers used as studding for homes and other buildings are commonly referred to as two-by-fours, but they are not actually that exact size. In fact, they measure considerably less than two-by-four inches—more like 1½ by slightly under 3½ inches when purchased. And even *that* measurement hasn't always been constant. What's going on here? Why the difference? The problem traces back to a piece of wood in embryo! It starts out as a stripling, rough-cut two-by-four, but gets trimmed smooth and is surface-dried to its present smaller size for marketing. The same holds true for finished two-by-twos, which measure similarly less than two-by-two.

U

ULCERS AND MILK

"Overacidity causes stomach ulcers; drinking milk neutralizes the acid!" That standard prescription has been given to the ulcer-ailer for years, but there is no evidence that milk has any mitigating effect on your burning ulcers. In fact, current findings reveal that cow's milk or any other kind of milk is likely to stimulate the production of even *more* stomach acid. Whoa!

UNCLE SAM

While it is true that the cartoon figure of "Uncle Sam"— America's national caricature in high hat, beard, and coat-tails—is quite lovingly regarded today, it is wrong to suppose he was always admired. The term *Uncle Sam* first originated as an *unfriendly* nickname brought about by the acerbic objection of people in New York and Vermont to the War of 1812. The name "Sam" derives from New York businessman

Samuel Wilson, who sold barrels of salted beef to the United States Army—Uncle Sam's beef.

UNDERWRITERS LABORATORY (UL)

What is the meaning of the UL logo, which appears on toasters, electric fry pans, and other electric appliances, and which is as familiar as your own initials? One interesting survey revealed that most people didn't really know, but they surmised it applied primarily to household appliances. Essentially, the UL logo is a sort of *Good Housekeeping* seal of approval that gives manufactured products a passing grade. What is generally misunderstood about the mission of Underwriters Laboratory is the extent and range of the products it tests. It turns out that toasters, frying pans, and the like are but a very small part of UL's diverse sleuthing program. Each year the UL stamp of approval appears on about six billion new products representing some 12,500 different types of goods—computers, aerial ladders, wood paneling, magnetic resonance imagers, tracer golf balls, upholstered furniture, modular homes, cleaning fluids, fabrics, stepladders, floor coverings, and a host of other things, including teddy bears and life jackets. So don't be surprised if someday you pick up a tissue box and find that UL has been testing the nose-blowing capacity of your lilac-scented hankies.

UNIFORMED SERVICES OF THE UNITED STATES

It is generally assumed that all persons authorized to wear official military-type uniforms are in some way connected with the *Department of Defense*, i.e., the Army, Navy, Air Force, and Marine Corps. But of the seven uniformed services of the United States, *three* are not under the Defense Department, and their members also wear military-type uniforms. The Coast Guard is a component of the Department of

Transportation; the U.S. Public Health Service is a part of the Department of Health and Human Services; and the National Oceanic and Atmospheric Administration is a Commerce Department agency. Symbols and customs such as salutes, scrambled eggs on officer cap visors, and addressing superiors as "sir" are as much a part of their mandate and tradition as they are of the fighting forces of the DOD. That's why Vice Admiral Joycelyn Elders, appointed U.S. Surgeon General in 1993, wears a military uniform and gets military-type respect from her counterparts.

U.S. MINT

Most of us are familiar with the term *U.S. Mint,* but it is surprising how many people are under the impression that the mint is responsible for producing *all* of the nation's currency—both coins and paper. The U.S. Mint is the agency responsible only for *coinage*; paper currency is printed by the Bureau of Engraving and Printing. Another misconception surrounding the U.S. Mint has to do with profit-making in coin production. Surely the U.S. government doesn't make a profit on the coins it mints, does it? Indeed it does! Profiteering in coin production is possible simply because the *monetary* value of today's "sandwich" coins is higher than the *intrinsic* value of the metals of which they are made. In addition to the coin-collecting hobby that brings in revenues of about $300 million to the federal government on numismatic sales, the mint adds another half-billion-plus dollars to the government's coffers in seigniorage, a wheezy term that defines the difference between the government's coin-production cost and the face value of the coin. The last report I heard is that the fed makes 0.4 cent profit on each penny manufactured.

UNITED WAY

America's principal charitable fund-raising organization, the United Way, is seldom regarded as a *business* by most people, but it is. Though chartered as a non-profit enterprise, it is nevertheless a corporation, structured in the Fortune-500 fashion of the big buck-makers with the usual corporate lineup of chairman of the board, executive committee, president and CEO, vice presidents, staff workers, and an indispensable army of trench workers, manning offices, battling the phones and fax machines, promoting their charity wares, and groping with the dispiriting business of collecting money from sources all too anxious to offer resistance. The free-enterprise model of profiteering has proven to be workable for nonprofiteering activities as well. So, whatever works!

UNMARRIED YOUNG MEN AND WOMEN
It is often heard that young unmarried *women* outnumber unmarried young *men,* resulting in more of the females being unable to obtain husbands. According to the U.S. Census Bureau, single guys outnumber single girls in their twenties by about 2.3 million. This supposedly is because many women in their twenties have married men over twenty-nine years of age. However, says the census, for those *over* age forty, there are far more unmarried women than unmarried men.

V

VATICAN
When referring to the Vatican, people generally regard it only as the spiritual sanctuary where the business of the

Catholic Church is conducted and which the Pope calls his home. Technically the word *Vatican,* when used alone, is a misnomer. Actually, it is a short name for the state or territory as a *whole,* and for the city of Vatican City, which makes up the state—the smallest independent state in the world. Containing 108.7 acres of land, Vatican City is all the territory that remains to the Pope of the former Papal States, which for many centuries included Rome and all of central Italy. The Vatican's official name in Italian is Stato Della Città del Vaticano, meaning the State of Vatican City.

VENUS'S FLYTRAP
North and South Carolina's Venus's flytrap seems to be one befuddled plant—looking like a plant but acting like an animal. Because of its name, many folks think the carnivorous plant eats only flies. Actually it catches more ants than flies, but will snap shut on anything its sensitive trigger hairs touch—but only if the trapped prey is alive as evidenced by *movement.* It can even be fooled into eating something else, like a piece of hamburger meat, if it is repeatedly stroked, giving the impression that a moving, lifelike prey is inside. Unsubstantiated stories tell of the flytrap capturing and digesting small frogs. The best guess is those stories came from a Muppet character named Kermit.

VESPUCCI, Amerigo
Another misconception about our America regards the gentleman Amerigo Vespucci, who, in 1497, supposedly planted his Italian feet on the soil of the New World and gave the continent its name. But Vespucci, born March 9, 1454, made no such voyage, nor did he ever suggest that the New World be named after him. By his own admission the 1497 voyage was a fabrication. Claiming he had invented a new lunar astronomy stretched the fabrication even further. The technique claimed was already in use in Vespucci's time. Then why was America named after him? Research suggests that a

beguiled mapmaker was responsible for the unfortunate misnaming.

VESUVIUS
Many poorly researched literary depictions of Pompeii's cataclysmal tragedy of 24 August, 79 A.D., leave readers with the impression that most or all of the citizens living in the ill-fated Italian city were killed when Vesuvius blew its top. Horrible as it was, with the enormous outpouring of ten to fifteen feet of lava, pumice, and ash that covered the town (in addition to the killing fumes), the mortality count was only 10 percent of the town's total population. Out of about 20,000 Pompeians, it is estimated that the actual death count was 2,000 souls. Moreover, the devastating earthquake that preceded the Vesuvius eruption by seventeen years actually did far more damage than the volcano itself.

VIPER
It is commonly believed that the word *Viper* applies only to a single species of snake, but actually, there's a variety of venomous vipers to be found. A viper is but one of an entire group of poisonous snakes found in many countries. Zoologists identify about 8 out of 100 snakes as vipers. Pit vipers are one major group, but even there we have several sub-families—rattlesnakes, copperheads, and water moccasins, all pit vipers, having a characteristic pit, or hollow, below and in front of each eye. Over half of the world's vipers have the pit. Remember, they are venomous critters, so don't get caught in the pit with one! Incidentally, not included in this family of snakes is the "vindow viper."

VIRGIN
The word *virgin* has several different interpretations, but the meaning it has today is greatly changed from its early connection. In Hebrew, the word *bethulah* used by pre-Christian writers suggested *an unmarried woman*. The Arabic

root means only to be mature, and the Aramaic doesn't connote sexual inexperience at all. It generally meant *one of marriageable age*. Thus the original meanings suggest that an unmarried girl could still have been considered a virgin even if she had actually experienced sexual intercourse.

VIRGIN MARY

Although classical artists have traditionally painted the Virgin Mary as an older person (her maturity born of their own imagination), Bible scholars and researchers mostly agree that Mary, the mother of Jesus, was but a young teen of approximately fifteen or sixteen years of age when she gave birth to her beloved son Jesus in Bethlehem's lowly manger.

VIRUS

Contrary to what most people suppose, viruses are not living organisms, at least not in the usual sense as we understand living matter. The qualifying criteria for determining what constitutes living matter is a substance's ability to *reproduce* itself, something the virus cannot do. That makes the virus somewhat of a freeloader, inasmuch as the only way it can reproduce is to invade a living cell (called a host cell) and borrow the cell's protein-synthesizing machinery to carry out its genetic messages. It is also incorrect to assume that viruses are "little cells"; rather, the virus is an independent genetic system capable of transferring itself from one cell to another. Also, it is often erroneously thought that there is only *one* virus that causes the common cold. Actually there are over 150 different types associated with the common cold.

VOICE, Sound of

Logically, it would appear that it is the ears that first pick up the sound of a person's own voice, but the sounds emanating from a person's own vocal chords are picked up *first* from the bones of the skull. The ears pick up the voice sounds three one-thousandths of a second later. (The ears get first dibs on all sounds outside of the head, however.)

WALDEN POND AND THOREAU

Where does one draw the line between a pond and a lake? Perhaps we can't. Consider Walden Pond. Most people who have only read about Walden Pond must be of the opinion that it is little more than a pollywog pond. This is far from true. Walden is at least large enough for small whales. When Henry David Thoreau built his chateau and opted for solitude on the outskirts of Concord, he probably wouldn't have considered a 62-square-acre, quarter-mile body of water to be a mere pond, and it isn't. So we have to put a little more water into his pond and make it a lake. The life of the mysterious Thoreau also leaves us with other misconceptions. For instance, was he the literary hermit that history has pictured him—away from all those dreaded humans? Consider this: Thoreau often entertained while at Walden. In fact, he titled a chapter in *Walden*, "Visitors," and many a day he traipsed the short two-mile distance to Concord for groceries. Actually, his whereabouts at Walden Pond were as well known to Concordians as everyone else's. It was also known that the land upon which Thoreau's cabin was built belonged to Ralph Waldo Emerson, who gave him permission to cut timber for the structure.

WAMPUM

It is a common misunderstanding that wampum, the small cylindrical polished-shell beads used as money in Colonial America, was used as a trading medium only among the North American Indians. Actually, wampum was legal tender for both Indians *and* palefaces, particularly in Rhode Island, until about 1670, and in New York until 1700. The funny money didn't fade entirely out of use until about 1800, as it was a very useful token of exchange for the settlers of that time. The trust factor for wampum wasn't as good as gold by any means, but in those frontier days a left-handful of wampum plus a right-handful of trust usually clinched the deal.

WASHINGTON, George—His Military Leadership

Certainly, George Washington, the father of our country, was endowed with myriad commendable traits and talents, but skill in military tactics wasn't one of them. He was not regarded by close associates as the superior commander and field general that legend portrays, and according to the Encyclopedia Britannica, he was "guilty of grave military blunders." Jefferson even characterized Washington as being "a failure in the field—not a great tactician." To John Adams, he was "an old muttonhead." Sour grapes in Washington's day?

WATCH JEWELS

Although we still refer to the minutely small bearings used to facilitate movement in watches as "jewels," we shouldn't expect them to have much intrinsic value. That's because they are synthetic, and have been for the greater part of the twentieth century.

WATER MYTHS

Mankind has been drinking the precious water that laveth the thirsty land from the *beginning*, whenever the beginning began. Too bad we still have a lot of hydro-hooey to unlearn about it—our shrinking supply, treatment policy, and pollution bugaboos. As to water abundance, it isn't true that we have less water today than a century ago. A water measurement a billion years ago would dip-stick exactly the same as today; we just use it differently today. We recycle it, pollute it, treat it, waste it, sell it, and distribute it, but it levels out the same. Another myth: When we boil water, it kills all pollutants. Actually, it doesn't! The boiling only kills the bacteria and other buggles; we could still be slurping up metallic pollutants and other inorganic impurities even after boiling.

WEIGHT LOSS THROUGH SWEATING
Bivouacking in sweat suits in the unbearable heat of health-spa saunas will indeed result in weight loss, but the loss will be *water* loss, not fat loss. Once fluids are consumed, the weight will return. Moreover, such attempts at weight loss can backfire, resulting in a net weight gain if fluid loss is replaced with calorie-loaded drink and food. So, if we want to lose weight, we'll still have to *eat less* and *exercise more*, and, of course, neither option spells fun!

WHEEL
From most everything written on the subject, the wheel was not a working implement known to the early Indians of North America. The fact is, they *did* have a knowledge of the wheel and used it, not on large useful conveyances, but on *toys*. Archaeologists, who have found wheeled toys among the Aztec ruins, tell us the absence of wheels for wagons and carts may have been due to the absence of beasts of burden to pull them.

WHITE TONGUE/CONSTIPATION
One of Aunt Priscilla's old remedies guaranteed the riddance of the white-tongue syndrome by the unscientific mixing of herbs, licorice root, and vinegar. But the wretched concoction wasn't intended for the tongue itself but for the constipation that was supposed to have *caused* the white, furry tongue. For those who still link constipation to a white tongue, it would be better to consult an ear, nose, and throat doctor for a more accurate diagnosis, because there is no

apparent linkage between the two. The doc will tell you that the cause of white tongue is the overmultiplying of living organisms that occur naturally in the mouth; it has nothing to do with one's prolonged toilet time.

WILLS AND THE PROBATE PROCESS

Despite how much has been written about wills and probates, it is still not uncommon for people to assume that wills do not have to be probated. That, unfortunately, is not so. Or perhaps it *is* fortunate in that the purpose of the probate is to prove that a will is genuine, that it is the true will of the deceased. Another thing about wills is that although (at the present time) most states have "right to die" laws which recognize living wills as evidence of intent, such wills may, or may not be, legally binding, depending on the state. *All* wills, however, can be challenged, except irrevocable wills. Additionally, people still feel it is mandatory that a lawyer make out the will. Not so! And finally, wills do not require notarization by a certified notary; two persons—whether they be semiconscious, sober, or indifferent—are all that is required to make a will legal.

WIND-CHILL FACTOR

Our garrulous TV weather reporters often talk about something called the "wind-chill factor," and suggest we button up our overcoats because the wind has somehow lowered the temperature outside. But does the wind really lower temperature? No! It doesn't! If there were no living things on earth, there would be no such thing as a wind-chill factor. So it has to be something else. The wind-chill factor refers only to the heat loss from *body surfaces*. The factor is calculated in calories lost per centimeter of the body's skin in a given time period. So whether the weather outside is delightful or frightful, the blowing wind just isn't going to affect the temperature at all. The wind-chill factor can indeed make it *feel* colder, but it's not something that a bowl of hot chili can't rectify!

WINDMILLS
Holland and windmills are so linked in our minds it is hard to realize the Dutch didn't have anything to do with inventing the big fans. The whole windy idea for using wind power in this manner dates back at least to the Persians at about 644 B.C., in Seistan, on the borders of Persia and Afghanistan. They didn't look like the colorful Dutch windmills we see today on postcards and in van Gogh paintings, but were of a more crude assemblage—in the fashion of sails attached to vertical-axis center posts that picked up the wind from either direction. Even the windmills of Europe and China antedates those developed later in the Netherlands.

WISE MEN
Christmas songs and stories all recount the story of the three Wise Men who traveled to Bethlehem bringing gifts of gold, myrrh, and frankincense to Jesus, the future King of the Jews. The problem with those accounts is that they lack validity. The Bible makes no record of how many Wise Men there were, the speculation being that there were three, each bearing one gift. Greek traditions say there were twelve, and other writings stretch that account to as many as fourteen. Also, the Wise Men weren't thought of as kings until the third century, and it wasn't until the sixth century that probable names were associated with them—Gaspar, Balthazar, and Melchior. Moreover, to which Magi do the stories refer, the Persian Magi, who were credited with profound religious knowledge, or the Babylonian Magi, who were often considered imposters? Some would question whether the Wise Men arrived immediately after the birth of Jesus. When Herod sent his hit men to Bethlehem to butcher every child under the age of two, was it because the soothsayers couldn't crystal-ball any more precisely than two years? It seems that Matthew's account makes it quite obvious that the Christ child was indeed a newborn when the Magi visited him.

WOLVES

Some of nature's animals get high marks just by being themselves, some don't. The much-maligned wolf has always received bad press from a largely uninformed public, and, unfortunately, children's books perpetuate their share of wily-wolf stories, especially stories like "Little Red Riding-hood," and "The Three Little Pigs," and Jack London's looney lore. In truth, el lobo is one of the most intelligent and socially sophisticated animals in the wild. Excellent hunters and devoted parents, they have little inclination to harass humans. Documented cases of wolves attacking and killing human beings are rare to nonexistent. Nor should we fall for that "full moon" nonsense either. Wolves don't engage in useless extracurricular activities like howling at the moon. They *do* howl when the moon is full, but they also howl when there is *no* moon, and they probably don't even know it's there anyway. Like all wild animals they're in it for food, sex, territoriality, and a bit of good old family fun (not necessarily in that order).

WOMEN AND WEALTH

Although it seems that men and money go together, it is the *ladies* who control most of it. It will undoubtedly shock the macho gender to learn this, but the gals own approximately 70 to 80 percent of our nation's wealth. Although in most families the man is the breadwinner and is primarily responsible for building up the couple's financial portfolio, he has the unfortunate habit of dying earlier than his spouse, and so the jewels go to the surviving widow.

WORDS

According to the Book of Genesis, at the time of the construction of the tower of Babel the whole earth was of one language and of one speech. The people then built that ridiculous skyscraper, supposedly leading to heaven, but which only led to the confusion of tongues, and which has confounded God's children ever since. Following is a limited list of words that confuse:

a. Ambulatory. A surprisingly large number of people connect the word *ambulatory* with the word *ambulance*—all those sirens and sensations of a fast trip to the hospital, all those people who are unable to walk. But the word has nothing to do with vehicular ambulances. On the contrary, *ambulatory* doesn't pertain to the *inability* to walk, but to the *ability* to walk or to move about, to not be stationary or bedridden, etc. Incidentally, the term *ambulatory surgery* carries the same connotation. It is called "outpatient surgery" or "same-day surgery," meaning a surgical procedure that doesn't require an overnight hospital stay.

b. Attila the Hun. It may be of small consequence that Attila the Hun, the great fifth-century barbarian ruler and invader of Europe, has his name invariably mispronounced by most everyone, but to set the record straight, the vainglorious avenger's name is accented after the double T's (Att'ila), which is masculine, not before the final *a* (Attil'a), which is feminine. No doubt heads would roll if the mighty "Scourge of God" were alive today and heard his name so blatantly mispronounced!

c. Bankrupt. Often this word is used as an adjective, describing a business misfortune, situation, or state, as in "The man brooded over his bankrupt business." But more correctly the word *bankrupt* pertains to an *individual*, a person who has been judged legally insolvent—as in "The poor bankrupt lost everything."

d. Diphtheria. The word *diphtheria* has to do with problems of the membranes in the throat that give rise to breathing difficulties. Most people probably don't know that, and those who do spoil it all by mispronouncing it. Phonetically the word is pronounced "dif-thir-ea," not "dip-thir-ea."

e. Encyclopedia. Why are there so many typos when it comes to the word encyclopedia? It's because it is spelled two ways. The Brittanica has it spelled "aedia" while the other publishers spell it "edia."

f. Enormity. The word *enormity* even sounds enormous, but it doesn't pertain to size. Rather, it indicates some form of evil, wickedness, or outrageousness. Could we then say: "The *enormity* of Antarctica is apparent from these maps"? Not really! How about: "The enormity of his evil deeds soon came to light!" Try it!

g. Mundane/Supermundane. Most of us are aware that the word *mundane* refers to things typical of the ordinary, the earthly, the worldly, the profane, and the temporal. But then we get confused with the word *supermundane*, thinking it means *more* mundane than *mundane*. Actually, *supermundane* is the antithesis of *mundane,* and means being above the world. (This word is also spelled *supramundane*.)

h. Papier-mâché. Those seemingly endless creations that arts and crafts buffs make and sell to other crafts buffs are made of paper-mache, are they not? Well, yes and no. First of all, they are indeed made of paper, but their proper name happens to be *papier-mâché* not paper-mache. The word *papier-mâché* is French and means "chewed paper."

i. Perestroika. It took a revolution to inveigle Americans into learning a couple of Russian words, but already they're being interpreted incorrectly. The new openness seen in the Eastern bloc countries is often referred to by Americans as *perestroika,* but the correct word describing openness is *glasnost*. Perestroika pertains to a restructuring of the economic, governmental, and political system within the "restructured" Soviet Union. And with that bit of trivia, you are now quite bilingual!

j. Progenitor/Progeny. It is easy to get tripped up on the words *progenitor* and *progeny* because both words have *people* and *families* as a common denominator. However, the words have opposite meanings. A progenitor is a direct ancestor or an originator of a line of descent; the word *progeny* refers to one's offspring.

k. Sensuous. The word *sensuous* is often used (mostly misused) to describe a person given to unrestrained gratification of sexual appetites—a carnal, voluptuous person. But the correct word for such a Romeo is not sensuous, but *sensual. Sensuousness* pertains to those qualities that appeal to the five senses—to the pleasure sensations, void of sexual lust.

WORDS AND MEANING

With all the wordsmithing going on in the last few entries it would seem prudent to put Mr. Webster aside and get on to something else, but an important aspect about words and meaning needs clarifying: Preposterous as it may seem, words by themselves do *not* convey meaning. Word *meaning* and word *usage* are two different things. The primary function of words—best described as language symbols—is simply to stimulate the nervous system into remembering past experiences; the word symbols are used to call forth whatever experiences our cerebral computers happen to contain in a selected area of interest. Every language (German for instance) contains thousands of words, but if a person hasn't *learned* German, then the words convey no meaning. If the person *has* learned German, he then possesses the symbolic tools with which to call forth his experiences. Try directing a Tokyo cab driver to a desired destination if he doesn't understand English. You will be using *words* but you may also end up in Osaka!

WORLD'S OTHER SIDE

It has often been facetiously suggested that if it were possible for a person to drill a hole completely through the world starting at some point in the United States, the person would eventually find himself in China, supposedly meaning that

China is directly *opposite* the United States on the big round ball. Suffice it to say, those who believe so haven't looked at a globe lately. Upon emerging from the long hole, the digger wouldn't find himself in China, but slightly to the south of the center of the *Indian Ocean,* thousands of miles from China.

WROUGHT IRON

Many people refer to iron that has been hammered as "wrought iron," and they are entirely correct in doing so. The word *wrought* is the archaic word for worked. But what is generally not understood is that a piece of wrought iron that has been hammered for a particular purpose—decorative lamps, for instance—was also called wrought iron *before* it was hammered. Wrought iron is one kind of three types of metal made from high-quality pig iron that has been mixed with a sand-based, glasslike slag to make the iron more malleable. Therefore, to refer to a piece of iron that has been hammered (or worked) as being wrought iron is correct, but it was already called wrought iron *prior* to it being hammered. Perhaps the greater misconception regarding the iron issue is that most people mistakenly refer to wrought iron as *rod* iron. (But then again, they too could be right!)

XMAS

Although the shortened, informal spelling of *Christmas* is often viewed as an irreverent merchant's gimmick, disrespectful to him whose birthday it stands for, a knowledge of the etymology involved should erase the resentment. The term *Xmas* comes from the Greek letter *X*, transliterated as *CH*, representing Greek *Christos*, or *Christ*. Most of today's hustling merchandisers are not privy to this fact, however, and even if they were, the name of the game is whatever rings the cash register!

Z

ZIPPER
Was the zipper something that was perfected in our day, as most people suppose? Are we talking about the thing (a hook and eye device with slide fastener) that Whitcomb L. Judson of Chicago invented way back in 1892? We are indeed! Later a man named Gideon Sundback modified and improved the crude hook-and-eye zipper by adding interlocking metal teeth. Judson's friend Colonel Lewis Walker obtained a patent on the zipper in 1913, and in 1924 the B. F. Goodrich Company gave the trade name "zipper" to rubber galoshes closed by meshed-teeth slide fasteners. A modern idea? Hey! Your zipper is considerably older than you are.

Postscript

For those who have an annoying misconception they feel they'd like to share, you are invited to send it in. I will reserve the right to include it in a future work with no more than a thank-you for doing so, but shoot, if we can put another fallacy in the fire it may reduce your stress level, and we'll both be rewarded.